Days Off in Oxfordshire

Happy Christmas,
Monica!

All my love,
Tem

x

2011

By the same author

The English Path
Tongues in Trees
Three Women in a Boat
Life with Art
Walking Aloud

POETRY
By the Harbour Wall
From Parched Creek
Snow Buntings at Barton Point
Goodfellow

Days Off in Oxfordshire

KIM TAPLIN

With illustrations by Rachael Sherlaw-Johnson

THE WYCHWOOD PRESS

First published in 2011 by
The Wychwood Press
an imprint of Jon Carpenter Publishing
Alder House, Market Street, Charlbury, Oxfordshire OX7 3PH

ISBN 978 1 902279 43 5

Our books may be ordered from bookshops or (post free) from
The Wychwood Press, Alder House, Market Street, Charlbury, OX7 3PH
01608 811969

e-mail: orders@wychwoodpress.co.uk

Credit card orders should be phoned or faxed to 01608 819117

Printed in England

to my grandchildren Tilly and Ruskin, hoping these places and others like them will be there when you have grandchildren of your own

PREAMBLE

I thought of calling this book "Days Out in Oxfordshire", as in "Shall we have a day out?", but also as in unavailability ("The person you are calling…") or, even more radically, "She was out of it." I wanted all those meanings. But in the end I chose "Days Off" because that carries a sense of leave, of stepping off the treadmill, of availability for ways of spending time and for thoughts one usually has to sideline owing to busyness. And also as in "Where are you off to?"

Although I've lived for nearly fifty years in the county, there are areas of it I've never visited. I've walked around West Oxfordshire where my home is, and made sallies elsewhere; but there is a greater abundance of beauty and interest than I could ever exhaust.

I get into a rut from time to time, as anyone can and most of us do, even if we are not on someone's pay-roll or being a full-time carer; and I've found that a day-trip with my bus pass and on foot to one of my favourite oases, or to somewhere completely new to me, can revive and nourish me almost magically.

The book came out of a dozen such expeditions in different months of the year. I wanted to share my observations, as any nature writer or any travel writer does, but also to suggest the benefits to the psyche of such simple undertakings. My impressions are personal and idiosyncratic: I am not for a moment presuming to speak for the places. In any case places run deep, back to prehistory; and we can rarely do more than scratch the surface, even when we focus on just one. All I hope to do is to impart some of the pleasure of these mini-pilgrimages, or mini-adventures, whether just to be shared from an armchair, or whether they set readers off on explorations of their own.

I've reached all of them by public transport and on foot. I'm lucky enough to have a bus pass, and in the case of the Warburg nature reserve I rather perversely took three buses when I could probably have got there more easily by train. Part of the fun for me was using the Traveline website, which is not perfect, but is still very useful for showing you how to get from wherever you are to wherever you want to go and back. I haven't included bus numbers and times. These change, and not all my readers will want to travel from Tackley. Besides which they may prefer, if they like the idea of such jaunts, to seek out places of their own .

For the most part, the places I headed for have some kind of geographical identity, are free to get into, out of doors, and free of cars. Having said that, you need to buy a pass to get into the bird hides at Farmoor (at the gate) or Standlake (at the Woodstock Museum), and Abingdon Museum is not out of doors. But hey – it's a day off; there are no rules, ok?

When my first book *The English Path* came out in 1979 it was generously reviewed by Ronald Blythe in the *TLS*. He identified the English footpath as an excellent, and free, prescription for body, mind and spirit. Almost all these expeditions involve some walking, often on footpaths, and the getting there and back was an important part of the experience. Footpaths are still my passion and my chosen means of access to the countryside, but I have also recently identified a desire to inhabit a place a little, even for an hour or two, to get somewhere and hang out for a while, just to be there.

This is a crowded island, as a recent visit to rural France re-reminded me. There are not many places here where such a deep quietude can be found, free of planes and traffic noise. But yet it is surprising how easily one can still find oneself alone – the concentration in towns and cities seems only to intensify.

There is no especial magic or holiness in the places themselves (although I want to say again as I have said before that we should do well to consider that all places are holy, and to act accordingly): nor are they a definitive selection. In writing about them I wanted rather to suggest the riches that are there to be discovered, the restorative pleasure to be had, in a hundred places in this county or in any other, to add my voice in thanks for the fact that they have been kept relatively undespoiled, and to hint at reasons why such places are essential to the nourishment of the human spirit as well as refuges for the rest of the natural world.

CHIMNEY MEADOWS

Cars swoop past on the dual carriageway with the deadly regularity of a bacon-cutter: slice, slice, slice. They butcher the peace into neat portions, and as if to make doubly sure they emit noxious fumes. When a tractor-and-trailer passes at an imperturbably slower speed, leaving a lingering smell of the dungy straw they are transporting, it is a sweet reminder that real life – rural life – still exists somewhere off the road.

Conversely, in the rural hamlet where I live, the sound of the rush-hour traffic a mile away, especially loud if the wind's from the south-west, reminds us each morning of that parallel world of presentation, and expense accounts, and haste. Usually at some point the urgent blasts of an ambulance up the pulse, reminding us that people regularly are injured and die in that rat-race. The quick and the dead. We recently had need of an ambulance ourselves; but it was a long time coming to our out-of-the-way house. The sat-nav had apparently pronounced that it could cross the River Cherwell from Kirtlington by means of a bridlepath, although even on horseback that is now too risky an enterprise. The old wooden sign, half-hidden in ivy, points through deep, swirling water beneath a weir. When the ambulance does find us, the paramedics are gentle and careful, They want to send their heart reading back to HQ, but they can't get a signal. The parallel worlds often thus find difficulties in communication. They speak different languages.

Today I am up by the A44 waiting for a bus. It's my first venture of this kind since I sat with my mother at the start of the year and the end of her journey. In her last few days she no longer ate or drank, and it was not even clear whether she waked or slept. She was in no pain. Only, she breathed. At times I fell to counting her breaths, how many a minute. Nights and days came and went and were breaths also, in and out. She was over ninety years old, and so had come a considerable distance already, and it seemed to me that her dying was work. As though she had to be patient and persevering towards that slow-coming goal, like someone tired at the end of an all-day walk.

Her increasing dementia meant I had lost her a lot earlier, bit by bit, but still I found that after she was gone I needed to grieve. And to brood. The great mystery had its hold on me also, and kept my spirit half-bound to its contemplation even while my body and mind went about their business of bagging up old clothes and having conversations with all kinds of officials across desks, and continually reminding myself that this was real, and that my own journey had therefore brought me to a new place. The little bus-and-foot pilgrimages with which previously I had refreshed and renewed myself seemed part of an earlier life. Sometimes even walking out from the house seemed a hard thing. In short, though it was spring in nature it was winter in my soul; and it wasn't till the world's summer was almost gone that I found myself almost ready one day to look outwards again.

And Chimney Meadows seemed a good place to begin, partly because, using public transport, it takes a bit of getting to. The nearest bus stop is in Aston, and from there it's an easy enough walk, along tarmacked lanes with little traffic, but a walk nonetheless, which helps deliver one's spirit there by degrees. It's often been said of air travel that it makes too rapid a transition for some part of one's being, and that because of that some vital element of true travel is lost. It seems to me that this applies right down the scale, that human nature is such that we find the value in places more easily, and appreciate them more, if we have taken our time – if possible a two-legged creature's proper, walking amount of time – to get to them. Partly it is that the journey itself may hold interest and nourishment. But partly it is that, whatever else it holds, the journeying gives us time to detach ourselves gently and thoroughly from whatever preoccupied us before, and to prepare ourselves, to open ourselves to what lies ahead.

I'd been to this nature reserve a few times, once with a friend at the beginning of August a couple of years before. At that time the geographical description from the leaflet was robustly brought home to us. When you spend much of the day wading, the phrase "Thames flood plain" ceases to be an academic matter. But my friend Val believes in enjoying life. With some companions the trip would have been voted a washout, but she didn't allow the water to dampen our spirits. The land-and-water-scapes had considerable beauty, getting to the hides had an extra spice of adventure, and above all we had that exhilarating, somehow liberating, feeling that nature is always going to be wilder than we can tame. We felt put in our right places, small.

This time a small, devastated notice at the entrance devastates me. Vandals, it says, have been onto the reserve, and among other things have let the cattle out "by the fjord". The strange mis-spelling of ford somehow brings home the unhappiness of the writer. The sanctuary had been violated.

Sometimes I wonder if there is not something about the very act of trying to make a refuge that rouses anger and the desire to destroy in poorly-nourished souls. In 1970, on a year in the States, I observed the hackings and daubings in Rock Creek Park in Washington D.C. – a public park, not the preserve of the wealthy. In fact I imagine the wealthy never went there. I was advised never to go there alone. It was notorious for muggings and even murders. In this country a mile or two from where I live I have seen saplings which someone had planted to beautify a public place each savagely hewn down. I understand that we are all responsible for the society we have made; and that if our own niche in it gives us a love of nature, a greater measure of content, a sense of community and more constructive ways of channelling our anger, even these things may in some way be gained at the expense of other people. So fences get higher, padlocks multiply, rotweilers threaten to rip people apart, and tribalism seems to be ever on the increase.

Meanwhile today is showery and breezy and I find myself relishing and being cleansed by the big skies and big clouds as you especially are in a flat, Dutch-painting countryside. Although the inflorescence of early summer has gone over, the meadows are full of flowers still. The slightly sinister yellow rattle, which grows here in abundance, is now at the stage of the rattling seed-pods. It is apparently semi-parasitic, which is I suppose why I feel it to be sinister, in the same way that fungi are. But then when all is said and done most of us feed off another's vital spirits on occasion: we are most of us semi-parasitic. And this plant, I understand from the leaflet, by weakening some of the tougher grasses, makes room for a great variety of other meadow plants to grow. Still in flower are yellow and purple vetches, black knapweed, red clover, and the pinkish bramble flowers, leading one's thoughts on to autumn fruitfulness. And there are still plenty of butterflies around, one of the delights and benefits of old, unsprayed hay meadows. I wonder, when they seem so fragile, how can they fly in the rain. But then, how do butterflies and little hollow-boned bundles of feathers like the warblers cross oceans? Strength and resilience is not always with brawn and heavy equipment, as Ray Mears, with his local moccasins and birch-bark canoes, delights to demonstrate.

Dr. Kerry Lock, who is the warden here, would no doubt be able to explain the science to me, of butterflies in the rain. We came once to follow her round the reserve and listen to her explanations, and marvel at her immense learning carried so lightly, and linked, as it seemed to me, with a love equally profound. Every now and then she would stoop to seek for or point out some tiny plant or beetle, knowing her reserve intimately. She drew no attention to herself, but led us out, into the real world that underlies the man-made. She gave the most powerful insight I have ever had into how things hang together: ecology. That hour or so walking round with a true scientist who knew and loved her patch did more for my deep sense of connectedness than any number of heavy books or hall-filling prestigious lectures. She walked lightly, she taught lightly. Am I allowed to say that she was beautiful? Certainly through her I could intuit something of an answer to my current butterfly endurance question, which it seems not quite possible to put into words.

The alternative way to the hides, through the fields rather than along the lane, is full of clover, and I am in clover, breathing it in, filling my lungs with that particular honeyed, wholesome-seeming sweetness. My daughter Phoebe, in the damp, dreary, dark and devastatingly cold Moscow winters, puts a scarf on her head and steps into one of the many churches. Though not a believer she is revived and heartened by devotion clothed in colour, light, music – and the honey-scent of scores of votive candles.

But what's this? Just as I am basking in sweetness and sunlight in a break between showers, here is a dark, matted hulk of flesh across the path. A dead badger. Already partly torn open by the cleaners-up after death, but nowhere near yet to whitened bone, this is a heavy and a bloody spectacle still, and a puzzling one. Usually animals that are not victims of us in our cars do not die out in the open. The smell of mortality is strong, and I don't linger to examine the creature. *Et in Arcadia ego.* I console myself that the fresh meat will have helped to feed some corvines, birds which Mark Cocker's gloriously obsessed book *Crow Country* has recently taught me to look at with more interest and respect. The clamour going on in a big tree on the far side of the meadow is from a bunch of young kestrels though, who sound like a cross between, say, quintuplet babies all woken up at once, and the sort of teenage party they will be having in a few years' time.

One of the reserve's successes has been the number of breeding barn owls, and they have made use of the huge nest boxes placed for them. But as these beautiful and ghostlike birds are largely crepuscular I have usually had to head for home before they appear. One time though, a family were picnicking and enjoying the place and the kids erupted into the hide with loud running footfalls on the planking and laughter, followed by apologetic parents. "No need!" we said with genuine, and not politely manufactured beams. Because a few minutes before they came a barn owl had flown past within inches of our faces, clearly disturbed by their excited approach. And they had seen it too.

Encouraging the natural delight of children in the natural world is not new; but it seemed to be somewhat in abeyance in the sixties and seventies of the last century. I remember rather wistfully recalling the "nature tables" of my own childhood, when nothing similar seemed to be on offer for my children. The glitch seems to have been part and parcel of a general sense that nature as now mastered by science was nothing to do with sticky buds and tadpoles but everything to do with labs and test tubes. At the same time, no-one with even a modest amount of money need have much to do with the earth. Food was packaged, clothes were factory-made and cheap, cities were where you had to work if you wanted to get anywhere. These are wild generalisations of course, and all the time there were far-sighted voices of warning and pockets of resistance. Now that we are beginning to pay the price of our soulless imagined superiority to nature, attitudes are changing again. Many schools again teach something about the natural world, sometimes even in a hands-on way with gardening and simple animal husbandry. And the larger nature reserves offer pond-dipping, and flower hunts and bug hunts and eco days for all the family. Programmes like *Springwatch* and *Autumnwatch* are hugely popular, and stress personal involvement in a way that is new.

A few years ago I was in a hide with a couple of old codger birders when a bunch of five or six kids came in. All watched the ducks peaceably enough, the children only a trifle more volubly, and then suddenly the flash of blue fire and a kingfisher perched a few feet away. One of the children let out an excited shriek. That child could have been playing a computer game, or hacking down saplings, but what did those evil old men do? Did they say, "Yeah! Beauty, innit?" or even "Cracking bird"? No, they growled and tut-tutted and told the kids off for making a noise. Now I might prefer a hide without added kids, or grumpy old crusties come to that, but just then I knew where my sympathies lay, and I could cheerfully have wrung a couple of scrawny old necks with their own scarves.

Sitting in a hide now on a rainy weekday, when the wind-moved branches scrape a little eerily on the wooden roof, I can indulge my pleasure in being solitary in the natural world to the full – and for the next two-and-a-half hours it is uninterrupted. Except of course that I am not solitary, because in the absence of other people the birds feel like company. The gentle rural poet William Barnes wrote that "trees be company", but I have not yet been able to follow him that far. Birds, yes. And on an uneventful, unspectacular afternoon such as this one each tiny event receives something like its proper welcome and appreciation. I catch my breath at the sudden rich rose of a bullfinch. I hold it in awe and delight as a whole family of whitethroats move through without haste among the foliage in the ditch just below me, keeping more or less together but taking their individual routes and pauses just as a human family may do outdoors, and conversing with each other (what else can I call it?) in small cheeps as they go. After a shower I am treated to a display of swallows and martins back and forth at speed across the riverside meadows, and then with no warning the rain returns and descends in a thick veil. It hisses down hard, and the birds hide themselves, or are hidden. I emerge when it stops into a fresh and dripping and glistening world.

As I walk back it is towards a baroque sky of prodigally piled-up clouds which seem to need fat Olympians reclining on them in loin-cloths. A walnut tree is equally prodigal with its green-jacketed nuts, and yet I never noticed it on the way here. Some people will only consider "a round walk", but I am always just as happy to return by the same route because I always notice new things. Like this lovely scent of lime flowers at the bend in the lane, a scent which the rain has brought out. And the wider views, naturally, are different. On the skyline now, to the left of the main village of Aston, and dominating the quiet unexceptional coun-tryside are the words BODY ROCK. I ask a woman walking her dog what it is, but despite being local she seems equally ignorant. "Sometimes it is all lit up," she volunteers. Perhaps she lacks the curiosity gene, because on hearing that I have been to the nature reserve she has a ques-tion for me: "What did you think of it?" Her tone manages to imply that she's heard it's not very good – no tigers perhaps, or flamingos. She herself it seems has never been to visit it, she and her dog. "I always turn round at the bridge," she says with an air of having proved an impossibility. (At the said bridge, I noticed that road signs had been thrown into the water. Plain old vandalism, or is it anti-motoring freaks like me, but from the direct action wing?) My inner social worker urges me to urge her to give it a go: "It's beautiful," I say. "It's not far at all." But it's fairly clear that for some reason she's set her face against it, and thinking it over later I kind of hope she doesn't go. She'd only be disappointed, and the dog might disturb the nesting curlews.

I am the only passenger on the bus back: I feel like royalty with my own driver. But please go to Chimney. It restoreth the soul. And go by bus, and crowd it full. If no-one uses the buses they'll stop running them.

WARBURG RESERVE

It's a fine, blue day with breeze and heaps of white cloud. Today's the day I've fixed on and kept clear for my first visit to the Warburg reserve, near Henley. Really and truly, it is too far for a day trip from Tackley using buses, but I feel challenged by the fact that this "flagship" reserve is at the other side of the county, and determined to give it a go.

It happens to be Hiroshima Day. For some reason, out of all the grim anniversaries one might choose to remember, I always, when I notice the date, involuntarily remember this one. I think it is less about the thing itself than that one year in my younger, peacenik days when I stood in a vigil in the centre of Oxford to remember, a coach-load of Japanese tourists happened to arrive. Seeing our banners they ran and embraced us, and stood with us, grateful, some even with tears in their eyes. We had no common language but needed none. It is the moments of something shared far below the level of normal social intercourse, or when the cara- pace of the social self is somehow withdrawn, that stay with us. This is probably what they would remember of Oxford, this unlooked-for meeting, long after the great colleges and the Bodleian library had melted into one historical blur.

On the bus to Oxford people sit silent, as the English mainly do. It is a national characteristic that has not yet changed, though there are several different skin colours. But then a mobile rings, and soon, with a jingle-jangle, another, and soon conversations are going on in more than one language. We have mostly taken to that strange carrying of our little worlds with us like an extension of our thoughts. It is not always pleasant to be privy to these snatches of someone else's life, but it seems to be accepted and not considered impolite. How quickly it has come about! I can remember the first time I ever saw someone use a mobile phone: it was a well-known writer, and he was standing in Radcliffe Square in Oxford. At the time, I hadn't even heard of such a device – they were not yet widespread – and it gave me the odd feeling of having strayed into science fiction. I half-expected them to beam him up.

The bus gets in late, but the one to Crowmarsh Gifford, where I have to change, is even later. The third and final bus is, fortunately, later still, so it all works out. Sometimes the drivers are so good-natured that you guess they see making people feel better as part of their job. It seems to go with knowing their route and feeling some benevolent ownership of it. I have known buses drop individuals at their own doors, and the friendly greetings and farewells make the whole bus load lighter. This one has got out of bed the wrong side. He doesn't know the turning to Bix, and the way he says so, and calls me Love, says plainly "and I don't care". Often it feels good to me to be called Love: it is astonishing how the same word can mean both friendliness and scorn. I loved being Petal on the buses in Cumbria, and that always seems kindly meant. Mr. Sulky here would like for me to get off at the wrong place, but with close attention to my map and some suggestions from another passenger, he is thwarted.

I swing cheerfully along the single-track lanes, plunging steeply down as though into the earth and then up again into the sky, because these are the Chilterns. I am grateful for the tall thin light-seeking beeches that shade my way, because it's turning out to be hot. Through the gaps you glimpse sunlit pasture and arable fields and red-roof farms in the dips, a scene very different, in a hundred small ways, from the farmland of my own patch in West Oxfordshire. We have few red roofs for a start. But there is also a groomed tidiness about the countryside here that feels foreign.

A striking blue flower like a wild Canterbury bell rings out its sky colour every so often from the dark earth beneath the trees. When I look it up later, it seems to me it might be nettle-leaved bellflower, which according to the book likes woodland and is the original Canterbury bell of the Elizabethan botanists. There are none of these in Tackley, and they contribute to my feeling of having travelled far enough for things to be foreign.

There is plenty of money in parts of West Oxfordshire, but somehow the Chilterns are moneyed all through – perhaps it is the nearness to London, the easier commute. There are a lot of horses. There are horses in Tackley too, but they seem humbler, more bucolic. Here the very dung has a shining and prosperous air, and the whinnying that mingles with the greenfinch's wheeze and the red kite's far-carrying hail sounds like repeated jackpots. If hardship exists here it is hidden. Credit crunch – what's that? It sounds like something you put in the pocket of your Barbour to snack on while hunting. But I thought hunting didn't happen any more? Did you? Well, you may be right. Or not. Alright, while you're hanging about at the point-to-point.

As for the red kites, they are undeniably thriving. And they are stunning birds. It's hard now to imagine the Chilterns without them, or to remember how relatively recently they were reintroduced. These days a Chiltern landscape seems hardly complete without one, leisurely a-sail in the heavens with its forked tail spread, or sometimes disconcertingly close overhead and showing their rich colouration and markings. They belong in the picture now, just as skylarks once did above cornfields.

There have been stories in the local papers about smalls going missing from washing lines and turning up in the kites' nests: what most people probably didn't realise was that it'd been going on for centuries. "When the kite builds," says Shakespeare's Autolycus, "look to lesser linen." So come to think of it the kindly Somerville librarian was mistaken in more ways than one, all those years ago when I was an undergraduate. I asked if there was anything on the Elizabethan underworld, and she mis-heard me – "Elizabethan underwear? I don't think they wore any, dear!" It may have been linen rather than nylon, and more serviceable than the lurid wisps you can buy now which scarcely seem, in the politicians' phrase, "fit for purpose"; but something there must have been to attract thieves whether human or avian.

I pass a stretch of elm hedge, amazingly surviving. I learnt on a guided walk that elm now never makes it above a certain height without succumbing to the disease, and that trees of full height are not to be expected; but I live in hope, and always feel cheered when I see some elm in which the corky diseased bark and too-early yellow leaves have not yet appeared. There's an apple tree in my garden that fell sick of something or other soon after it was planted, probably as a result of my ignorance and inexperience. That was forty years ago, and at first it produced only small scarred and misshapen fruit, which soon rotted. But after about thirty years it seems to have recovered. Its apples are sweet and juicy, and if not quite supermarket quality-control standard, they are nonetheless good to eat. Perhaps the same thing, some immunity perhaps, may happen to the elms, those shapers of an English landscape my children can hardly remember and my grandchildren have never seen.

Out in the open once more, and the verges are full of flowers. When you look closely there is a miniature garden of yellows, blues, pink and whites, with the occasional accent of a poppy. I can recognise melilot, bindweed and speedwell, also various cranesbills, white campion and big white daisies. This plant with yellow flowers, close-set up a straight stalk, what is it called? The name agrimony comes to mind, and when I look it up later that looks right, together with the fact that it is said to be found especially on chalk. That's what the book said: my editor, who is clearly a better naturalist than I am, says it grows in this part of the county too, especially round Ditchley.

Valley Farm is handsome in its flint-and-brick coat, and with its weathered red-tiled barns and out-buildings, and it accommodates a good-sized colony of house sparrows. Huge sunflowers almost dwarf one of its cottages. I am always pleased to come across house sparrows: they used to enliven my hamlet too with their chirpings and little skirmishes, but as from many places now they are inexplicably absent, even though my house is a Noah's ark of other species living in holes in the pointing.

Footpaths tunnel away or climb in both directions. On the right, on the Oxfordshire Way, there are big clumps of wild marjoram. "Sweet marjoram" was mad King Lear's password, and it still grows on Dover Cliff where the end of the play is set, in a little flowery oasis close to a fast road. Like Edgar's talk of footpaths and bridleways, and Justice Shallow's orchard, it reminds us that our greatest poet came from the country, wherever he may have ended up.

The wayside grows still more colourful, with bright orange fruiting lords-and-ladies, mauve scabious, and the big yellow-green umbels of wild parsnip. I think. The leaves look parsnippy. And when I look it up that evening that seems to be right! Maybe I am finally getting at least the more common plants into my head. Once again it is one that likes chalk, and the book also warns about the possible irritant effect of handling the leaves in bright sunlight. This reminds me of being surprisingly asked last year, when I was working on an organic farm, if I was allergic to parsnips. Apparently one worker had been dramatically affected the summer before. Giant hogweed, from the same family, has a more notoriously evil reputation.

By now to stand for a moment under the shade of an oak is bliss. Everything is humid and still: the hot countryside is holding its breath. A jay calls hoarsely from the beechwoods above. A post van passes, and one jeep headed for the farm, but nothing else: the road goes, as we say, nowhere.

Which is a good place to be if you want to soak yourself in rural peace and forget for a while about cities and money and cars and human violence and greed. To the charge of sentimentality and escapism I plead: not guilty. Anyone writing with love about the countryside is liable to incur it. But even if one has not witnessed the sudden deadly slice of the sparrowhawk through the garden, or the squabbling around a bird feeder, many of us have watched the mortal dramas that modern wildlife photography brings to us as we sit on the sofa. Maybe it is immorality rather than blood that is so wearisome to the soul. Wordsworth wrote:

> *One impulse from the vernal wood*
> *Can teach you more of man*
> *Of moral evil and of good*
> *Than all the sages can*

But this hasn't prevented many thousands of would-be wise words being expended on trying to explain what he meant. Richard Jefferies, our greatest nature writer but out of fashion, longed to be able to bring city-dwelling factory workers to sit under an oak and renew themselves.

I can't put it better or clearer than Tolkien, who contrasted the escape of the prisoner with the flight of the deserter. When I walk out of my door or wave my bus pass to get into some nature I gain my freedom, move closer to the given.

The man-made world holds us prisoner, and its devotees hunt down those who try to escape it with the envious malice that is unconscious revenge for their own thin lives. In Aberdeenshire recently I came across the story of Charlie the Hermit, who in the 1920s had made himself a hoosie – a hut – against the rocks on the shore near Cullen. For thirteen years he lived there, eating rabbits and fish and vegetables of his own growing, but eventually he had to be hounded out by the authorities. You can still find the stone edges of his plots among the bracken. More recently a man lived in a shack in woodland, I think in Gloucestershire. But someone peached on him. There was a piece about him in *The Guardian*, telling how he studied the moths and other wildlife. He too was forced out, a man who did no harm, and who was probably anything but well-equipped in any sense for our so-called civilisation. But no, he must be made to have plumbing, and join in the rat-race. There are many such stories, and most of the complainers and disrupters of such people probably do more harm to the planet before breakfast each day than their victims do in a year.

Nature reserves are not, of course, wilderness – or not the small-scale ones we have in this country. But they do offer sanctuary from human despoiling to some of the other life-forms that share this earth with us, and make some attempt to provide them with favourable conditions of life. And in the process, increasingly, they are providing sanctuary for us. Particularly it is a relief to escape the noise and fumes and stress of cars, but less obviously there is respite for our souls in the absence of the obvious signs of human society – houses, shops, factories, streets. The focus here is other.

"Welcome", says the notice at the edge of the reserve – always a word that eases the heart. "Take only photographs. Leave only footprints. Kill only time" runs the now familiar mantra. As a worker with words I want to quibble a little: I don't take photographs anyway, but I do take away a heart and mind recharged. And killing is not something I would ever want to do with time. But I get the idea.

There are one or two other people in the small visitor centre, but when I head for the nearby "wildlife garden" I am alone. I park my bum gratefully on a wooden seat, and begin the next phase of my unwinding, enjoying a pleasant mix of satisfaction at having made it here, delight in my surroundings, and anticipation of my lunch. It may not seem much: old lady with bus pass gets it together to spend time outdoors. To me it is wealth and ease – of the kind that money can't buy.

As you sit and begin to re-arrange your agenda to receive life rather than to project yourself into it – as is necessary for action – you see more. Partly it is a matter of freeing up all your faculties for observation. (Except those needed to stuff your face – though even that can be distracting, as you look down to hold a wildish sandwich together, and drop crumbs into your binoculars.) Partly it is that wild creatures, which probably took cover as you arrived, will soon, if you stay quiet, resume their inhabiting of the place. One by one I clock up the birds as they flit to and fro between leafy hiding-places or visit the feeders: chaffinches, blue-tits, the always rather nervy and sudden inruption of a great-spotted woodpecker, the quiet and more self-possessed marsh tits.

Next I turn my attention to the butterflies, which I know less well. Like the flowers, I have to attempt to re-learn them each summer, and still that is only the most common and obvious ones. On a birding trip to Southern Spain we came suddenly and with a gasp of delight on a swallowtail basking on high ground, and I recognised it from a paper replica in my grand-daughter's bedroom. My pleasure in later seeing them at Hickling Broad, one of their few hang-outs in England, was again ecstatic. They liked to sit on the flowers of the wild irises, yellow on yellow. I wonder what makes people have a "favourite colour"? I look awful in yellow, and would never buy a yellow garment, but I love the colour in nature – yellowhammers, brimstones, primroses, buttercups, the polleny-looking yellow feathers of bluetits. It may have to do with my mother's liking for mimosa, which when she was feeling happy – or maybe to help herself to feel happy – she would sometimes, although we were hard up, buy from a barrow in the street.

There are plenty of butterflies here, encouraged by the deliberate planting of species that will attract them. The buddleias are the chief draw, those easy-going purple-spired recolonisers of railway sidings and scrapyards, with their strong distinctive over-the-top scent. They represent hope. They come where other plants mostly will not, enterprising survivors, re-greening: and butterflies love them. I can see large whites, peacocks and commas: with difficulty I have progressed thus far. My friend Val loves butterflies and has pursued them through the fields and commons all round Stonesfield, where she lives. The trouble is, the more you pursue them, the more they fly off. She took me out with a net once, and we had a great time trying to creep up on them to temporarily catch and identify them. It was good sport, and we laughed a lot at our own antics, but I can't say it was a great success as to increasing our knowledge.

Something catches my eye. Something a delicate, soft orange, larger than a tortoiseshell, scarcely larger than a peacock maybe, but less square, more elegantly shaped, I can't put my finger on it…something different. In a second, and without thought, without reflecting what a new idea this is, I train my binoculars on it, and can see its lovely markings in detail, and realise, from my brief glance at the wall displays in the visitor centre, that it is almost certainly one of the reserve's special species. I have never knowingly seen one before, and am inured to not usually seeing whatever unusual thing is to be seen. I am nothing much of a naturalist – as will by now be obvious. I have come to see whatever I do see, and to drink the juice of the place. But I go back into the centre with the lovely image still fresh on my retina and learn its name: silver-washed fritillary.

So that was what today was about. Every day has its high spot and low point. Today was the day I first saw and fed on the beauty of the silver-washed fritillary as surely as it was feeding on the nectar of the amethyst flowers, and what is one grumpy bus driver compared to that? Suddenly, undeservedly, gratefully, I experience life as a glass-half-full person – in fact, I would go so far as to say my cup runneth over. And what is more I have discovered binoculars as the way to watch butterflies.

It is too late in the year for most of the orchids, and I have too little time left to try to seek out the few remaining. I had heard the warden giving people complex directions earlier, and felt certain I'd manage to miss them anyway. So much always deliciously remains for another time, and my pleasure is undiminished as I walk the circuit through the woods. It rains just a few heavy drops and no more. Always the kites cry weirdly from on high, and on the path is a huge black beetle with a rich deep blue, stained glass blue, underneath. A sparrowhawk passes low across a clearing, and I can hear the unhuman laugh of a green woodpecker. Here are the – to my eye – somehow waxy flowers of autumn gentian, five-pointed pink stars. Or possibly (when I check on this later) it is Chiltern gentian?

Inevitably, I miss the bird hide, and have to go back and search for it. There is public access to most of the Wildlife Trust's reserves, but there seems to be a policy of low-key signposting. If you are really keen you will seek it out; if you're just looking for somewhere to down a few beers and frighten the horses – well, the birds and small mammals – you won't be attracted. Hides have occasionally been places of resort for teenagers. In Thatcham, where I once spent some time on a writing commission themed as a "Welcome to the Summer Birds", a hide had actually been burnt down, and hides were now locked, and you had to ask for a key. This reserve is much further from anything urban, and maybe here it just a wise instinct not to put too many labels or notices, but to let people discover things for themselves. Nature trails that are over-interpreted can lose all their magic, and feel more like a zoo. Plus you spend more time reading the boards than you do looking at the nature. The same thing goes for an over-explained art exhibition. I discover the hide and sit for a few minutes – all I can spare now – overlooking a small pond, and am rewarded by an immense stripy green dragonfly. I am aware that I have a seriously uphill stretch in my mile or two back to the bus, and will be seriously stuck if I miss it.

Time seems to race as I head back, but I find reserves (that word again) of strength and speed in me I didn't know I still had, and somehow I outrace it, climbing aboard beetroot-faced and sweating and triumphant. If they'd witnessed that last lap (which involved a small but crucial gamble on a short cut) the council would have indignantly confiscated my bus pass, which is for an old person.

FARMOOR RESERVOIR

To see a few corvines having a go at a buzzard is a fairly common sight in the skies round here, but today from the kitchen window I see something for the first time – two blackbirds on the lawn mobbing a magpie. They alternate in taking lunging nips at its hindquarters, dodging in to one side or another of the tail, and each time it gives a clumsy little jump and moves a step or two but stays, as though ruffled but somehow puzzled, as though its tormentors were invisible. It is all I can do not to shout out "Behind you!"

Of course it has to do with inveterate enmity, and the grim matter of egg-stealing, but outside the breeding season I like to imagine it's merely a kind of pastime. It makes me smile anyway, and I feel a welcome surge of gratitude that nature which so often lifts my spirits with beauty and awe can make me smile too.

I've been stuck in the house too long, slightly agoraphobic, but now there are Men In, and even though one of them is P.J., who has been doing stuff in my house for so many years that he's become a friend, and the other is his son-in-law Martin who is smiling and quiet, I am fleeing from dust and thumping and sharp painty odours: out has become more of a sanctuary than in. When I witnessed the birds' pantomime I was in the process of making myself a sandwich, which I planned to eat in one of the bird hides at Farmoor.

It's a muggy, overcast day, but the hide will shelter me if it should rain. Like a lot of people I have a thing about huts. There was a beach hut in Brightlingsea, where my parents lived in the sixties, and where the boyfriend and I went to swot in the long vacation. *The Battle of Maldon* is pretty dry, but the jammiest, freshest doughnuts ever could be bought in the village. A bag of these, boil up a kettle and sit looking at the sea with soft black Essex mud squidged up between one's toes and life seems pretty good. Later there was my twice-weekly "out-station" when I was a Registrar of Births, Deaths and Marriages, the Methodist hut behind the Manse in Kidlington, where on quiet days I could watch a gang of starlings stabbing ripe pears beyond the window. You could almost see the juice run down their beaks. Sometimes on walks I have come across sturdy railway huts still standing, each with a small stove, left over from when the navvies laid the track, and they too call up my simple-life/hermit/outlaw fantasies. For six weeks a little wooden "A-frame" was once mine when I led some writing groups, on the shores of the beautiful Christina Lake in British Columbia. And every now and then I spend a happy hour or so walking round the huge collection of huts and summerhouses at the Yarnton Garden Centre, planning which one I will buy. I haven't yet gone for it: I always end up telling myself I have more rooms than I use inside the house.

But what creates this longing? If anything could make me believe in past lives (which I don't) it might be this hankering for a wooden shelter – it has to be wooden – with some kind of natural view from the window. Surely I have once been at home in such a place? In fairy tales it is sometimes, though not always, where the good folk live. Sometimes it is the witch, who can be scary but may be useful. When I did those exercises that were all the rage at one time, a "guided fantasy" of going across a field, over a stream, etc., and eventually arriving at a building in a clearing in the middle of a wood, it was always a hut that I arrived at. We would usually have to go in, in our imaginations, and see what it was like inside, and eventually the workshop leader would reveal that "the house is the self", and we would all feel suitable things and have important revelations because our house had had no doors, or no windows, or was cold, or full of people we'd never met before…you get the idea. And there may be something in it – certainly I am not the only person to be disproportionately troubled while work is being done on my actual house.

It was many years before I discovered bird hides, although I have been interested in a very childlike way in birds ever since my aunt and uncle gave me *The Observer's Book of British Birds* for my eighth birthday. I still have it, stained and dog-eared and with the spine come off, and I now have several more comprehensive and grown-up field guides, but none more loved. Like Rory McGrath in *Bearded Tit* I relished the Latin names, but I lacked the intelligence to get it about habitat and migration and rarity: I was a slow learner at this as about everything else. The hoopoe, for example, appeared as a British Bird and so I was always on the lookout for one. I have now encountered *Upupa epops epops* but it wasn't till I was over fifty and in Mallorca. Astonishingly, they were camouflaged – so apparently gaudy as they are, pink with black and white stripes and sometimes a crest – against brick-pink earth in the dappled light under orchard trees. Later still I watched them from the roof-terrace of my daughter's flat in New Delhi, along with the same screaming green parakeets as you now get in London and the Thames Valley, and a surprising number of other species making a life among the traffic and pollution. My greatest fear was that one of the huge circling raptors would take an interest in the new baby.

As I walk over to Tackley to catch a bus, a great spotted woodpecker calls, and then I see it. It's one of the few calls I recognise, but I am trying to increase my knowledge. A friend urged it, he said: "When I walk I know they are there, even if I can't see them, the place feels friendlier". It was he who once tipped us off about a nightingale – "a particularly good singer", he said, and so, again at over fifty, I went to hear it, and it was my first. A lot of people mistake a thrush, or even a robin, both of which will sing at night, for a nightingale. They belong to the same mellifluous family, but this bird at any rate was in a different class. I'm sure if Shakespeare had heard this one he would not have said it was "no better a musician than the wren". We took a tent the next night, and fell asleep to the sound of it, and woke again at dawn to find it still singing, and it was one of the happiest experiences of my life. Another time we took a friend, who had never heard one before either, but she was unimpressed. But then I am not enthusiastic about grand opera. I am like

Christopher Sly, the tinker in *The Taming of the Shrew*, who is dressed as a lord while drunk and put to watch a play. He enjoys the attention and the booze, but yawns at the entertainment: "a very excellent piece of work – would it were done!"

The head of a deer moves across through the crop, and then the creature becomes aware of me and bounds springily and swiftly away. It is taller than a muntjac and more graceful. I must ask my wildlife guru, an elderly avatar of Robin Goodfellow who never seems to get older, what kind it is likely to be, next time he comes walking by with his dog.

In Oxford I change buses and head for the top deck front as my friend Diana taught me. Spying over fences from a height is a perk of the poor: the posh who never go by bus have nothing as tall as this! It is worth the steep climb, and puts me in mind of Lear who proposes entertaining Cordelia and himself in prison with gossip and philosophy "as though we were god's spies". It isn't necessary to own to enjoy, which is one of the reasons I take pleasure in public footpaths and allotments.

There are allotments to be seen from the top of a bus down the Botley Road, and lime trees, and big stores, but today I am distracted by a fellow passenger who throws himself a little intrusively into the seat next to me and commences at once to speak: "Don't like Oxford. Not like it used to be. Only stayed twenty minutes. Looked at some CDs. Cheaper in Witney." He is quite young and I think has some kind of disability. There's something a bit unusual about his speech, and his lack of reserve. For a few seconds I felt threatened, but realised almost at once that he was probably the more vulnerable of us two. I answered him quietly, and couldn't but agree about Oxford. I'd stayed for even less time than he had! He had some kind of pass and I showed him my Senior one, and he said "Oh, you've got one too," as though it made us mates, which I guess it did. When we said Cheerio and I got off, I felt cheered. He had no shell to speak of, was close to being "unaccommodated man" (Lear again) – "the thing itself" – and that can feel such a relief.

The path runs parallel with the road but separated from it by trees, which at this time of year are covered in small fruits, either red or yellow, which are also strewn invitingly on the ground. I am not sure if they are plums are cherries, or even if they are edible. I'd like to ask someone, but who would know? Who is my phone-a-friend? I know someone who would claim to, who is also rather reckless. He bites bits out of raw fungi to prove his bush-cred, but I'm not quite able to trust him.

Matt Prior might know: not the cricketer, but the Farmoor Wildlife Officer for Thames Water. I've been to a couple of talks by him, and I am his number one fan. He has a dry, almost hidden sense of humour and an air of total commitment. On one occasion he spoke about tree sparrows and his work to recover their numbers. Tree sparrows (like much else in nature) don't like a countryside that is too manicured. They favour tumbledown buildings. Birds after my own heart. Always as he spoke the birds were at the centre of the picture and not himself, but even so a picture of him emerged, as he went about constructing and placing nest boxes and topping up seed, and sometimes taking his family with him. When he was appointed to Farmoor he spoke to the Oxford Ornithological Society about his plans and priorities, and about how he was happy if rareties showed up, but that he aimed to make the habitat more attractive to lovely but less newsworthy birds – such as whitethroats.

One's feeling about a place is always coloured by any personal associations, from the faded brilliance of a single event to the weathered complex nuances of an old painting. Farmoor is where my erstwhile father-in-law spent his last months, in a nursing home, and my mother-in-law in a bungalow in the village, and although I have long been divorced from their son, I can never go there without thinking of them both. We took "the Da", as he was known, up to the reservoir once in his wheelchair. He liked the outdoors, and he loved the sea. But it was windy, as it often is there, and even with blankets he couldn't stay warm. Oxford is about as far from the sea as you can get in England, but after his stroke it was felt that the Da had to move from his Dorset house to be closer to where his family could visit. To see such a decided and lively man unable to choose for himself or even to speak very much was a sad and sobering thing. Somewhere in the Old Testament, I think, is a verse with one of those biblical contrasts, something to the effect, When you are young you can do as you please, but when you are old they will lead you where you do not wish to go. It sticks in my mind, but I can't track it down. Eventually, I do: it isn't in the Old Testament, but in John 21:18, and I can't for the life of me see what it's doing in the context, but it haunted me nonetheless, like much else in the scriptures.

My sadness is overlaid by the stored pleasure of many impromptu birding trips there with my partner Jeremy, at all seasons. If we take the car it's only twenty minutes away, making half a day an easy option, if the weather and our mood suddenly invite.

I love the windiness of the place, partly because it gives me a feel of the seaside. It makes for good sailing and wind-surfing, both of which happen on the water we drink, and make a merry spectacle of coloured sails and vanes. My son sailed here a few times with his school, and it gave rise to a lasting family joke regarding my slight deafness. He nudged me one day in the Cornmarket: "There's so-and-so" (I have forgotten his name) "he's a bow-tie salesman"! "*Is* he?" I said. "How unusual! Is it a Saturday job?" What he had actually said was, "He sails in the boat I sail in". Since then everything I don't catch and have to have repeated, calls forth affectionate groans of "Oh, bow tie salesman!" A trip to Farmoor always calls up that too, and a smile, and memories of younger days.

As soon as I walk up the ramp to the edge of the reservoir and feel the wind and see the sparkling water something lifts inside me. Yet the vast concrete basins with the tarmac causeway between them are not hugely picturesque. And there's usually unpleasant-looking scum and slime along the edges. The fetid-smelling liquid laps against the grey concrete, with a mess of feathers and faeces and sometimes even a dead gull. This, processed, is our drinking water. Since Jeremy first saw this he has bought water in plastic bottles, despite my murmurings about the cost, and the cost to the environment; but he ignores me as he has every right to do (it is one of the secrets of our success), and I go on drinking from the tap, so I suppose I am not completely lacking in trust after all.

Today there are boats out and whipping along, with orange, white, green and red-and-yellow striped sails. A beautiful athletic boy with long hair, surely a junior water-god, leans out from his boat and smilingly asks me the time, and then shouts encouragement to the kids in his charge. He must be supernatural, or why has he not got a sportsperson's water-proof watch? He reminds me of a similar good-natured youth who taught my children to swim in the Woodstock pool. "Call that butterfly?" he teased them. "It's more like dead moth!" But with none of the sergeant major's scorn, only a joking attempt to bring out the best.

This is the quiet time of year for birders: in fact I am the only one here. The warblers and other summer migrants have mostly gone, and the wintering ducks not yet arrived. I enjoy it all the same, and compile my nerdy little list of every species, including mallard, and pied wagtail, with as much relish as if I had spotted a rarity. Well, no, that's not quite it: if I had spotted the rarity for myself I would be delighted. But almost always I have to have whatever it is pointed out to me, as proper birders are usually happy to do, and I struggle to pick out – for example – the one gull among many that to them is so excitingly different, and I am not always sure I've succeeded, though I usually add it to my list, because I probably have seen it. Doesn't mean I'd know it again. When there are fewer birds I appreciate those that there are more thoroughly. There are hirundines still around, though not in numbers. I identify swallows, and both house and sand martins.

As I walk down the slope to river level from the far end of the causeway towards the Pinkhill hide I catch a movement in the grass and get my binoculars on it – a rabbit! Not a bird as I had hoped, but it adds a rural touch which I'm glad of. And from the hide I watch a number of butterflies, mostly whites. I can hear subdued bird calls mixing in with the sound of branches brushing in the breeze against the hide roof. It is peaceful to sit alone (in a hut) and watch the reed-fringed water of the scrape and the bushes and trees beyond, and I stay some time. This is the nearest I get to meditation, which I'm told is very effective, but which to me is like a car journey to an unwilling child, just are-we-there-yet? boring.

The walk alongside the Thames from Pinkhill hide to Shrike Meadow hide often adds quite a few birds to my list, especially in late spring when the warblers have arrived and all the small birds are to and fro feeding their young, and in winter when the leaves are off the trees. Today there is not much at all, but I enjoy the variations in mauve and white – purple loosestrife (Ophelia's "long purples"?), willow-herb, and ox-eye daisies and various white umbelliferae, as wondrously and mathematically constructed as snowflakes, and the dark clusters of small tight alder cones, set off by the round, deep green leaves. The river runs brown-green and slow. The big stand of reeds bordering this next scrape make a papery rustle in the breeze. I pass the place where the (once you've learnt it) unforgettable explosive notes of the Cetti's warbler can often be heard. These birds are localised, and fairly scarce, but are present here all year. Nothing doing today though. It comes on to rain and I wrestle my hood up. Then a flash, the briefest glimpse of a kingfisher, gone so quickly it is almost subliminal, but a reminder of how fiery life is always only hidden, even when our spirits are low.

Don't expect to see a shrike from Shrike Meadow hide. It was named from a great grey shrike that once spent some time there, and bears rather touching witness to the excitement and pleasure it gave to the birders who saw it. In fact, you have altogether a rather limited view, which can be frustrating. You have reeds and willows a few yards away, but the waters of the scrape are mostly hidden. They can be viewed from a third hide, on the edge of the reservoir, but at a considerable distance, or from a gap in the hedge. There are a couple of feeders, one to either side, which sometimes attract reed buntings, but they are often empty, and the reed buntings having bred are off in a flock elsewhere along the Thames. I have seen a flock not far from here, near Wytham, on occasion, and once near Tadpole Bridge. In spring and summer the great thing is the warblers. Rarely still and so needing a lot of watching to distinguish them, there are nonetheless so many so busy that the sport of listening to them and looking at them, and learning to tell a reed from a sedge warbler by sight and by song, can keep you as amused a long time.

Today the feeders are empty and so are the reeds. I munch on my sandwich and apple and sit tight, feeling just a little flat, though in general much better for being out of the house: and what, at this time of year, did I expect? Every other birder has better things to do today. Then something lands on a small bareish sapling to the right of the reeds, sits long enough to be seen, flies out, hawking, and back, and I can clock its warm brown back – and its white throat! Matt Prior would be pleased, and so am I. It stretches its neck up as though for me to make quite certain, then flies across into the sallows, then into the bushes behind the hide, then back again. And suddenly there is something else, very close. It is distinctly grey in comparison with the other bird, a lovely silver grey, and it too has a white throat. I write this down, to look up later. A proper birder would know what it was straightaway – I had a good view. When I get home I tell Jeremy, and he says: "What about a lesser whitethroat?

That's grey." And I look in the book and there it is, unmistakably what I saw a few feet from the hide, and all the more exciting because it's usually a bird more heard than seen, singing from the shelter of a bush. This feels incredibly satisfying: so often one rushes to the book, whether flowers or birds, and turns the pages with increasing puzzlement and frustration because nothing seems to fit the bill for what seemed as though it must prove obvious.

But Farmoor has one more gift for me today, and it saved the best till last. As I make my way back across the causeway, I veer from side to side, keeping an eye on both margins. Though apparently anything but tempting, the water's edge here, the little slimed concrete corridors against which laps the dubious opaque water, are often the place where a passing wader or two will choose to rest during migration. There are nearly always pied wagtails, and at one time a water pipit (not even included in my Observer's Book, any more than the Johnny-come-lately collared dove or the ring-necked parakeet) seemed to have decided this was home. Their movements catch your eye and they have to be checked out. But, oh look! Something else! A dainty wader with a black bill, about the size of a starling. Oh, and another. And two more. Approached slowly they are not too quick to take wing, and when they do it is only to land again a few yards behind me, as though merely wanting their own space rather than in fear. By now I have counted eleven altogether. I know these: they are dunlin. They are one of the commonest wading birds, but exquisite, in their varied and varying plumage of patterned browns and blacks and greys, and in their self-possession. Ten or eleven: they move about feeding and I lose count continually.

I was once on a guided birdwatch when a lone birder was watching something through his telescope and beckoned us over. It turned out to be a dunlin. Our leader thanked him but privately tsked at our party's being deflected for such an ordinary bird as it was in that coastal habitat. But it is good to enjoy the expected bird in the expected place: the lark's on the wing and the snail's on the thorn. We soon learn to grieve if it goes missing. My delight at the occasional house sparrow that still shows up in our garden a couple of times a year is as great as that at the occasional buttery yellowhammer among the chaffinches. These dunlins, or dunlin, as the "no s" plural seems to be of most waders, were not in the wrong place exactly, but were just passing through. In a few hours – days at the most – they would be gone. No-one had noted them in the log book, I was fairly sure they had not been there on my outward walk a couple of hours before, and there were no other birders around now. Even the sailors had gone. It felt as though I were witnessing the temporary, unpredictable visibility of fairies or angels. And because there was no-one with me I had to contain the excitement and delight in my own heart, a concentrated nourishment.

These birds belong at the sea's edge, whether on sand or mud, and so they bring into Oxfordshire a breath of coastal wildness, as well as the journeying thoughts that accompany all migrations. Not much about, the proper birders would have said. Enough though, to send me home happy.

CHOLSEY MARSH

"I'm standing in Tackley station which has got nothing at all!"

I heard this curious remark into a mobile phone as I also waited for a train. I remember the station when it was Tackley Halt, and had a waiting room, with a real coal fire in it, where Ivy Robbins, the station mistress, sold us our tickets. And it is true that now, on that platform for going North to far-flung Banbury, there is not even a shelter; so that you can begin, say, a holiday in Scotland soaked to the skin before you get anywhere near the peat and the whisky. But somehow I don't think she is remembering those days: I think she means cafes and shops, and I feel quite defensive about our station. After all, it has a platform, and that is more than so many places that fell under the Beeching Axe, driving so many more of us onto the roads.

It's a still, sunny October morning but it rained a lot the day before, and I decided I needed wellies for crossing the two wet fields from my house, and that since I was heading for a marsh they might be useful all day. I shuffle them a lot in the damp long grass behind the platform to get the worst of the mud off, but I still feel a bit of a yokel among the town-dressed folk who are heading for Oxford.

In Oxford I change trains. While I wait on the platform some

Americans appeal to me to interpret the announcement for them. I have considerable difficulty myself, but I manage it. One of the problems of ageing is that while some life skills are comfortably under one's belt, new ones are needed. Not just technology – there are courses for that – but the language. As a writer, this galls me. I enjoy slang and the language of the old Prayer Book in equal measure, and I like to move democratically between them. But increasingly I need my grandchildren as translators.

We move off along the Thames valley with here a deer and there a drift of Michaelmas daisies, and soon I'm getting off at the – to me – completely unknown station at Cholsey. I've passed through it many times. Once, memorably, I watched a middle-aged woman get off and be lovingly embraced by a middle-aged man waiting on the platform. They walked off together hand in hand, and imagination filled in a quiet, romantic, very English idyll which attached itself to the place. Cholsey! What a desirable place to live!

It soon became clear that a very large number of people were about to test the truth of that fantasy. A long suburban road of twentieth-century houses and bungalows, some a little shabby, eventually led on to a lane, Ferry Lane, soon sloping promisingly downhill. Some men in safety helmets were shovelling hard and some were standing around watching, in that way that always seems inequitable. Perhaps at intervals they swop over. This was the site of Fair Mile, the Victorian lunatic asylum, soon to become the site of many new homes. The hedge on the left sports the highest density of "Private, keep out, no access or public right of way" notices – in various colours – that I've ever seen; and being a walker I've seen a good few. Such overkill inevitably provokes curiosity: what is going on that is so absolutely not to be investigated? I read later on the internet that there is an equally phenomenal amount of security surveillance, so that the fact that – the station loos being unaccountably locked – I had to sneak into the hedge for a pee is probably on blurry record somewhere.

Later I browsed for some time among websites fascinatingly chronicling the history of the asylum, showing photographs of the decaying buildings by someone who had managed to stay beneath the radar, and setting out the planning proposals and the opposition. My mother in her middle age spent time in a mental hospital whose buildings were of the same period, and reading about this one stirred up my usual sludge of pain and frustrated inability to "define true madness". Now it seemed this area was to be "developed" for the sane, although there were those who had tried to object that this course was madness, in view of the lack of local provision for a good life…

Among the too-early browning horse chestnut trees were a few sweet chestnuts. These again reminded me of my mother when in her happier days she and my father would take me walking in Richmond Park and we'd come home with a bagful to roast on the fire. I don't know whether they are still to be had there, or whether perhaps those were a particular variety, but these and others I see always seem too small to bother with.

Ahead of me are puddles the width of the track in which a pair of wood pigeons are bathing and a blackbird drinking. The wellies which have been feeling rather hot and heavy suddenly earn their keep by taking me through dryshod, and there ahead of me, at the site of what was once the ferry crossing, is the Thames, and to the left a gate into the riverside reserve. A boat slides across the bottom of the lane, giving a pleasant sense of the river as a highway.

On the opposite bank a lawn comes down to the water's edge. As a girl I used to fantasise about living in a house with just such a riverside garden, with a rowing boat moored at the end. It had to do with my mother's liking for boats and for going to Stratford-on-Avon to watch Shakespeare, both which pleasures she communicated to me. I had no understanding then of the politics of access. I now know that such properties almost always interrupt public access to the river bank, and I believe, with W.H. Hudson, that we have a kind of natural right to walk alongside a river, as too along the coastline.

Here there are only one or two lawns, and for the most part beyond the further bank gently rising autumnal farmland stretches away in a faint mist, with distant red tractors turning the earth and a scatter of white gulls feeding on the newly-exposed grubs.

The river is slow and dark green. No-one else is about. Mallards swim placidly by. It is I who disturb a moorhen I hadn't seen, which skates across to the far side without really taking off, leaving a panicky wake.

Yellow willow leaves slip down, but otherwise there is little movement. In this stillness I am even more than usually inclined for a seat, and behold! a single, sturdy, comfortable wooden one offers itself. What did I do to earn this? Once I am sitting, basking actually, in the Indian summer sun, my thoughts too begin to settle, and I can give myself more fully to the experience of being where, in more than one sense, I have aimed to be.

Those who practice meditation may possibly smile at my inexperienced fumbling after what they are adept in. Or not. Not smile, or maybe I haven't grasped the concept of what it is they aim to reach. I wish for the tranquillity to become aware of the other. I am not good at tranquillity, but neither have I ever got on with meditation, was never really drawn to it. Once or twice in my life I have briefly attempted to be part of a group that practised it, someone having persuaded me it would be beneficial. Now though, sitting on my seat, the seat that yesterday rested and tomorrow will rest other grateful bodies and souls with their individual bent, I am entering a blissful state with what I begin to see is the speed of long practice.

I have written elsewhere a poem in praise of public seats. I love them for many reasons, not least the publicness they share with rights of way, but perhaps chiefly for their invitation to step aside from the rat race and enjoy the view.

There are alders. My creative friend Diana once gave me a birthday present with an alder cone as a beautiful flourish to the wrapping. I didn't even know what it was! I have an October birthday, and so the hedgerow harvest of shiny brown conkers and gleaming red rosehips are somehow especially pleasant to me, but alder I had missed. Now, I look out for them in their watery habitats, and here the clear green of this year's tight round cones contrasts beautifully with the black of last year's.

Suddenly speed enters the stillness. Twenty or thirty hirundines appear, to twist and turn in the upper air and then swoop to skim insects from close to the surface of the water, feeding up for their migration. Across the damp umbels and other browned plants one or two flying beetles move too, but in a kind of autumn torpor. Mechanical noise sounds distantly from that site that soon a lot of people will call home, and I can also hear the mewing of an unseen bird of prey. Dragonflies and damselflies are about in numbers. As usual my inner critic tells me I am too lazy/useless/unskilled to identify them, but today I sidestep this debilitating parasite fairly easily. Yes, I say. But aren't they lovely, in their hovering, quivering, jerky strangeness? And look, those two are mating. A bird flies fast and low upstream along the middle of the river, but I am too slow to stand up and identify it. It could have been a cormorant – there was a hint of black and a paler shade.

I get out my lunch and watch the changes in the sky. Big cloud masses have appeared, and the sun is now in and out. When it is out, long gossamers gleam across the path, and mallards, and dragonflies and certain leaves glint too: the whole drabness of dying vegetation looks full of life. Every mote on the surface of the slow green river is picked out by the light. A girl comes jogging past in a white vest with her thick honey-coloured pony-tail tossing. A small breeze starts up and the reeds speak a little.

A single, slow wasp comes to investigate my jam sandwich. I am glad something besides me still likes jam. Jam-making used to be a key autumn activity for me, and seasonality in all manifestations is a thing strongly woven into my psyche. But the demon sugar increasingly deters people, and I feel increasingly anachronistic. They still want my marmalade though.

The jogging girl comes back with her legs muddy, and she's rubbing her arms as she goes.

"Cobwebs?"

"Yes, and thunderbugs," she says. "They're all itchy!"

The Wedgewood blue sky now has a long spine of white. Several helicopters pass intrusively over, one of them a cumbersome thing like one of those double buses you get in cities. I suppose they are practising to make our streets safer, or something. I remain unconvinced.

I decide I had better explore to the end of the reserve. I can always come back and sit some more. My friend Jean used to say that bird-watchers – as they were then called – could be divided into "arsers" and "twitchers", twitchers being those who like to go in search and arsers being those who prefer to wait for what comes. Nowadays people tend to refer to "birders", rather than "birdwatchers", and the term twitchers is kept for those who will travel a long way at short notice to add another rarity to their list. A landlady in the Scilly Isles told us a story of a friend of hers who had fourteen guys staying, and had just served up their evening meal, the meat and two veg were steaming on their plates, when one of them got a bleep or a text or something, whereupon they left the table in a body and were soon being airlifted to Scotland… It sounded like a tale that had grown in the telling, but you get the idea – it's obsessive. The years are inclining me to arsing more and more, but I try to keep a balance. Jeremy, if he leaves me sitting somewhere and goes exploring further without me to double check the identification, always comes back with news of an exciting bird I've missed.

This is obviously a hot spot for birds of prey. From my seat I've now seen four buzzards and two red kites in the sky at once. Walking along I am overtaken by a small troupe of long-tailed tits. Rose-hips hang picturesquely over a gate, contrasting beautifully with the faint mauve of Michaelmas daisies. There seem to be two distinct shades of the wild form, one only a notch mauve up from white, and the other a little stronger and more blue. Both are beautiful. I wonder if they are spreading, or is it merely that by some benign faculty or failure of memory one is impressed anew each year, as people often say they never saw so many berries as this autumn are on the hawthorns, and doesn't that mean there will be a harsh winter to follow?

Pink yarrow, like white flowers rinsed in blackberry juice. Huge, bloomy sloes. Small galaxies of dancing gnats and single, small, day-flying moths. A great-crested grebe quite close that isn't aware of me yet.

The next gate tells us to Beware of the Bull, but it is perfectly clear that there is no stock at all in this pasture beyond the end of the reserve. I go on a little way, to make use of the public path and to show myself (there is no-one else around to prove it to) that I am not to be deterred by landowners, and I then turn back into the damply aromatic and reedy reserve, headed for my seat again. In a brownish draggled waste of dying greenery, two dandelions are little suns. A single silver fish leaps from the dark river. A wren ticks low down near the water's edge. A woman comes by with a spaniel that splashes in after her thrown stick, and stirs up that fetid, sweetish Thameswater smell.

No-one has taken "my" seat, and I bless my good fortune again. Small natural events nourish me like good food. A flock of fifteen or twenty lapwings fly over high up, going quite fast, seeming to follow the line of the river. They break into two groups for some reason that's unclear, and then re-unite, as though flying round an obstruction. They are among my favourite birds in flight, their lovely lapping flight, dark and light, appearing on occasion almost to twinkle, free but controlled at the same time. A single white butterfly is still flying among the brown teasels, like one of the few remaining flowers of hedge bindweed taken to the air.

I have been thinking that several hours beside the Thames ought to have produced a kingfisher, and wondering a bit sadly if they are in decline. With a fraction of my mind I even foreshadowed honestly saying so in writing, that I failed to see one, as Richard Jefferies did when he went to listen to the nightingale and didn't hear it. People speak of a god-shaped hole in their lives, and at this moment I am aware of a kingfisher-shaped one. And after all, when Jefferies mentions not hearing the nightingale you do still hear it in your mind. But then three sharp high notes penetrate my consciousness, and I turn to look before my mind can produce the identification, and a sharp steely blue dagger rips through the scene as though from another dimension. I am vouchsafed an instant only, but it crowns the day. Time to go home now. And I'm not making it up, any of it.

STANDLAKE COMMON

On a November weekday forecast to be fine, I set out for Standlake Common. Taking advantage of a lift, I skip the Tackley bus and find myself at a Woodstock Road stop in Oxford a little early – twenty-five minutes early, in fact. With no book and no seat, I am very much thrown on my own resources to pass the time. Waiting for the bus at the Green in Tackley I usually watch birds. It's surprising how many species I can sometimes clock up – a pied wagtail on a roof ridge, sparrows in the guttering, a blackbird on the Green itself pouncing on a worm, a robin singing somewhere close, great and blue tits on people's garden shrubs, jackdaws and rooks flying over, a grey-brown collared dove, blending in with the Cotswold stone. In summer the quiet scene is dramatically enlivened by swooping swallows and house martins and the screaming weirdness of the wired swifts.

In North Oxford this morning there seems not much in the way of wildlife, not in the front gardens anyway, but the human life is interesting. Those on foot or on bikes are presumably fairly local, and I begin to realise that "North Oxford" – shorthand for middle class professional with money and probable university connections – is only one strand in many. A plump woman swings past self-consciously, heavily defended in makeup, with a bell-like skirt and a colourful knitted coat. These and her cigarette give her a somehow old-fashioned, and possibly an eastern European look. A man with an enormous ponytail of unruly black hair and a silvered beard bikes along at speed but unhurriedly. He looks purposeful and at ease with himself. Unlike the man on the opposite side of the road who loiters near the stop but never catches a bus. He can't be waiting for a particular one, like me. At this distance from Oxford any bus will do. The southbound stop is a bit further down, but he keeps staring at me with what, even from here, seems like paranoia. Maybe we both believe the other to be "loitering". There used to be an offence of "loitering with intent": I haven't heard the phrase for a long time. But this poor fellow's problem, and something indefinable about his body language says he has one, seems to be loitering without. He is killing time.

Jeremy was recently bemused by a notice in the waiting room at Birmingham's Moor Street Station: No Loitering. He is a law-abiding man: "What else is one supposed to do in a waiting room?" he wondered a bit anxiously. Moor Street is deliberately retro. It is also has a notice in the Gents, apparently, recommending that you "Please adjust your dress before leaving." It wasn't aimed at Grayson Perry (who perhaps is allowed to use the Ladies anyway?). It meant flies. Though these days, when there is such a lot of underwear on view, it would be hard to sustain an objection. But that was another world, wasn't it?

Another bicyclist comes by, with a minute child seated behind him, mini-helmetted, who nonetheless stretches out a tiny but clearly practised hand to press the crossing button. And then there is a small, quick-moving man in a fluorescent tabard, deftly pincering rubbish with a special implement. Cans, fliers, plastic bottles, paper hankies, tickets, wrappings are upped in short order and transferred to a plastic sack held open in the other hand. He works as intently as a bird, and I am reminded how quickly any birds of the crow kind will clear the lawn of our offered leftovers. He has got his job down, as they say, to a fine art, and to one of my temperament it looks preferable to the noisy, rough camaraderie of the refuse carts. But it is probably less well paid, and certainly not by the sackful. In some countries people would stare at such employment. One of the things my daughter has had to learn to try to ignore, living in Delhi and then in Moscow, is the rubbish that defiles streets, parks and river banks. Here public opinion has not managed to prevent it, but has decided our taxes must deal with it – at any rate in a place like North Oxford… This man is a good worker, and may have chosen to work outdoors. Wouldn't it be more rational, more satisfactory altogether, if we took our litter home and he could work at growing vegetables?

The bus lets me down at the Mulberry Bush School in Standlake, where children who have suffered emotional damage are helped to heal. It has always a quiet atmosphere, among its trees, which are always full of birds. It sets me thinking about army nurses in a situation like we have at present in Afghanistan, about the compassion of healers, but about the craziness of it, of human beings dealing with the damage deliberately inflicted by other human beings on their own kind.

With the luxury of a weekday, when most people are doing the necessary and unnecessary, harmless and harmful things that are all lumped together as work, I am alone as I start along Shifford Lane, as soon as I have got beyond the electricity crew who are putting up a new pole. As soon as I can I step off the track for a pee, glancing anxiously right and left and hastily adjusting my dress, but although this is part of a defined local trail, lovingly waymarked along its route with mosaics of woodpecker, kingfisher, pheasant and other creatures, made by local people, there is no-one about. There is plenty of fresh horse-dung, though.

It is still overcast and slightly misty, and there is that kind of damp cold that on a still day can seem colder than wind. I feel very thankful that I decided, right at the last minute, to wear a fleece under my waterproof. We've had a long and lovely autumn this year, but it can't last forever. These deliquescent inkcaps are on their way out, and even the few late wayside flowers of white campion are the exceptions that prove the rule. The trees and shrubs forming a tall mixed hedge alongside the lane give birds plenty of food and cover. I can hear them, and it's enjoyable (if chilly) to loiter a little and wait for them to show themselves. Through a gap in the trees there is a greening field of winter wheat, in which a huge, quiet flock of greylag geese are feeding.

Long-tailed tits have a variety of ways of announcing themselves, a gallimaufry of ticks and mousy squeaks and trills as on a miniature washboard. Almost always they are in small groups, slipping through the trees in a kind of continuous wayward dance which allows plenty of room for individual *jeux d'esprit* and gives the observer plenty of time to recognise them. They are not shy, only constantly active. Some strains are pinkish, mixed in with their black-and-white, but all have the same tiny round downy bodies and long tails, making them resemble airborne tadpoles. Harder to clock are the winter thrushes – are there both fieldfares and redwings? Very often the flocks are mixed, but to be sure one has to catch sight of a bird at rest for a moment, and recognise the blue-grey, speckled and rusty-chested plumage of the fieldfare, or alternatively the sandy eyebrow of the redwing, or, better still, its fiery, beautiful, beech-leaf flank not quite hidden under the wing. It is sometimes hard to find reasons to love November, but for me the slightly elusive splendour of the redwing is one of them. The fieldfare's sometimes more erratic flight, acting wind-tossed even in still weather, and their loud chacking calls, can be a giveaway. These thrushes bring in the season, arriving restless and greedy for berries, but as time goes by they can settle, on quiet winter days, into a quieter mode, peaceably feeding in a pasture so that you may not even see them until something spooks the whole flock and they take to the air and the trees. Or they can sit still in a big tree, or in several along a hedge, sometimes surprisingly unseen considering the absence of leaves. I've been seeing them for a few weeks now, but not, where I live, in such numbers, and not yet staying put. These particular old hedges, with a good mix of berries, seem to be a favourite resort. In spring and summer their place is taken by warblers – chiffchaff, blackcap, whitethroat – tuneful but even harder to see among the foliage.

My path is to the right at a T-junction, where I have just now seen a rabbit's white scut vanish at a not-too-worried lolloping pace. It is narrower, and the bushes are closer, but you can tell that at some time it has been a more important thoroughfare, because of the stone "metalling" that shows here and there. And it is still used by riders: I follow the horse-shoe prints in the mud, feeling lucky. Another flash of white rump, and then another: this time it is bullfinches, flying ahead of me, but not far. They are skulkers for the most part, with a dislike of open ground. This kind of thick, shrubby mixed hedge is their territory, and although the flash of white is often the first and last you'll see of them, they are not about to leave.

Some instinct makes me glance over my shoulder and a large fuzzy fawn dog, clipped absurdly, is coming along behind. Bugger. It looks harmless enough, but it's probably enough to scare the birds, and presumably its owner is behind me as well, and will want to overtake my slow, marvelling progress. But the horse-shoe luck is with me: the creature is too fluffed and shampooed to attempt this path, and it turns off down the track I've just walked. It is a long way from nature, this dog. It looks like an eighteenth-century dandy: I am definitely a country bumpkin beside it. I have just been reading Gertrude Jekyll's disgust with the equivalent in breeding show plants in the same way, pointlessly, out of their natural shapes. She was eloquent and took an authoritative, high moral tone on matters of taste. In our time of the ascendancy of celebrity chav, it is hard to do much except murmur.

Despite the season there is a lot of green, or I should say of greens – from the dark ivy through the pretty well perennial green of brambles to the vivid lime green of the sodden moss along a fallen tree. On one side of the narrow band of scrub are caravans, but perhaps they are used mainly in summer or at weekends, because no-one seems to be about. The loudest noise comes from the ubiquitous woodpigeons, which never seem to leave any perch without great agitation. It can have nothing to do with weight: contrast their clumsy take-offs with those of a silent, focused bird of prey – a buzzard, say. The pigeons always make me think of unnecessarily busy old-fashioned housewives, forever shaking out the bedding or the mats. They are always in a flap.

Occasionally there is a muted honk or quack from the still water of the recreational lakes, won, like all this area, from expired gravel workings. Honking or quacking can be loud and challenging, but this only serves to underline the quiet. One of the tributes to my father comes to mind, from a schoolboy of about nine in the primary school where he helped, at the end of his life: "He used to say 'Yo!' to me, but softly, when he met me in the corridor."

Unseen webs brush across my face from time to time, and a few insects are still a-dance in the beginning-to-be-wintry air. At the next turn in the path is another of the small mosaics: this one has the words "Time to Stand and Stare". Amen to that. Although sometimes sitting and staring can be even better, and having a key (purchased for not much at the County Museum in Woodstock) I prefer to go a few yards further on, turn right between concealing fences and along the slippery boardwalk, to the North Shore hide. Here I can sit and stare till everything in me slows down, and perhaps escape from a new noise that's snuck up on me – a fierce humming and fizzing from an electricity pylon. I seem to remember hearing that time spent in close proximity to pylons and their overhead cables is really bad for you. And wasn't there a character in a Thurber story who thought that electricity could come out of the plugs and get you? He would have got the hell out of here straightaway. I try to remember if pylons always make this noise, or whether it's just more noticeable on a still day on one's own. (I checked another day: they don't.) A couple of pigeons are sitting on the bars without apparent ill effect, but then they always do give the impression of being pretty stupid birds. Maybe something to do with the size of their small heads in proportion to their fat bodies. I pass quickly into the hide – which is empty and dark and smells pleasantly of timber.

There are two anticipatory moments when you arrive at a hide. The first is when you open the door. Will there be other birders in there, and will they be friendly? Will there be room for you at all? Or will you have the luxury the slightly cynical Andrew Marvell imagined:

> *Two paradises 'twere in one*
> *To live in paradise alone.*

That was misogyny of course, whereas my feeling encompasses both genders very even-handedly… I am only part-serious. I have had many friendly and informative encounters in hides.

Probably the most memorable occasion was when the hide contained a nine-year-old boy and his mother. The boy was bursting with knowledge and enthusiasm, fizzing like the pylon. The boy's mother gave the credit for his passion to his father, but she had brought him there – his father wasn't present. It set me thinking about the chancy business of trying to share your own enthusiasms and pass them on, without producing a determination by one's children to avoid them at all costs. I could produce examples both of apparent success and failure from my observation of friends and acquaintances, but can see no reasons for either, no common pattern. There are famous families of musicians and actors, where I suppose an entire way of life is involved. I recently read of the large family of a naturalist who lived in extraordinary conditions in pursuit of their father's work, and grew up to be naturalists themselves. I suppose that for the young people that life seems to be life, seems to be what you breathe, the planet you live on. Perhaps it is also in the genes.

The other thing about that boy is that he was black. In this country, despite our racial mix, it is unusual even to encounter people of colour walking in the countryside. Walking organisations are doing their best to reach out to "ethnic minorities", to show that the beauty and interest of the whole country, and not just the urban places, is open to them, and it is to be hoped that the situation will gradually improve. Just recently I was at Oxford station carrying my walking boots, and was accosted by a black guy keen to know where I'd walked – along the Thames from Eynsham and across Port Meadow to end up in Jericho for supper. It had been a great idea for my friend Deborah's hen party. He said wasn't it a bit flat? I said, well yes, it tended to be flat along a valley. He said he was going to give the Ridgeway a go next week. Great! So maybe word is getting out. But I often think about that confident, effervescent boy and hope his interest continued. It had to, really, it was rooted in him already, and I hope and believe that by now he is passing it on to others.

Today I am alone. Once inside and enclosed in aromatic stuffiness, there is the second revelation. What will I see when I lift the first flap, trying to do so quietly? Will there be a visiting glossy ibis? Will there be any birds at all, or will there be a cheerful team of guys in waders managing the environment, so that it will be birdy another day? Where shall I look first?

Today as I sit myself down to stare, there are too many birds to count. Too many for me to count, that is. Real birders can apparently count in thousands. I don't even know how they can be so certain about the smaller numbers, putting neat records in the hide log books. How do they know it isn't the same ones swum to a different place? I feel some affinity with the rabbits in *Watership Down*, who above a very small number had only a single word that meant "several" or "many". I believe there are also tribes of humans who think in this way, and I'd feel at home with them.

Slow to learn as always, it was long before I could tell one duck from another. Even now I have difficulty with anything but the full male breeding plumage – and even then it can be iffy. I can still remember the thrill of realising that a great tit was sometimes a coal tit. This will seem really strange to anyone with a good (normal?) eye for detail and a brain apt to record and classify. I was able to register tit-like behaviour, and a general idea of colouring. I think I thought that the not-so-brightly coloured and slightly smaller birds were females or juveniles. Finally I noticed that, whereas some birds had a distinct badger-like white stripe up the back of the neck, some only had a pale blur. I think laziness comes into it, but I believe I also have something akin to dyslexia when it comes to observation. The compensation is that the pleasure of identification has gone on for longer. I now find it hard to imagine how I could not recognise coal tits; but I greet what I privately call "badger tits" with a particular warmth of inward salutation, in apology for having earlier overlooked them.

But the ducks. I have at long last learned to recognise – in addition to mallards – half a dozen different species regularly seen in this country: the black-and-white tufteds, the wigeon with their pollen-yellow fore-heads and kitten-like mewing, the gadwall quiet and elegant in Quaker grey, the pochard with their three distinct colour areas – tawny head, dark breast and grey mantle. I have had to learn that the little fast-flying teal are not waders, that shovelers are not mallards with extra big beaks, that goldeneye are also black-and-white as are tufteds, but differently so, and lower in the water. The lovely greenish eider I know too now, from holi-days in their coastal haunts. Sometimes I am gripped with a kind of dismay: what if I had gone to my grave without ever coming to recognise those wild and wonderful birds beloved of St. Cuthbert? The saint drew close to them in his solitude and must have known more about them than almost anyone in that time before systematic, scientific birding. There is a wooden statue of him in the cloisters of Durham Cathedral with an eider at his feet. And then, of course, I start to think about all the birds – just the birds, for starters – that I have never even seen, that I'm probably going to miss this once-only opportunity to know before I do take my last breath, and it saddens me more than any other category of thing that probably I shall now never do.

If that is so important to you, why not become a twitcher? you might ask. My answer is that that might be quite fun, in a list-ticking kind of way that I do indeed have a touch of, but it is not what I am talking about. This that I mean by coming to know a bird can go deeper and deeper of course, and never be finished, but it certainly can't be achieved by a single sighting, however dramatic. Some people lean so far the other way that they become followers and lovers of a single species, or a single family. We once met an Austrian couple on a boat, who gave off a quiet sense of joyfulness. We got into conversation with them, and they told us that they spent all their holidays following the cranes; and having later seen, and particularly heard, their wild, thrilling skeins for ourselves, we could see what drew them.

Partly it is a matter of personality. Some people make friends fast, get stuck in, see a lot of someone, ask a lot of questions, tell a lot in return. I almost always want to take things slowly. I act as though I had all the time in the world. I look forward to a slow ripening, and it doesn't always happen. I suppose it connects in some way with being a slow learner. And it is the same with birds. It takes many sightings before I begin to be familiar with that ineffable thing that birders call jizz, a sort of de-spiritualised version of haecceity, or thisness, before I can recognise the bird as one can an old friend, even from the back, even in a crowd.

Partly – wait before you tar and feather me, sisters – it is being female. In matters of bird identification I automatically defer to men. It's self-perpetuating: I expect they will know more than me, and usually they do. Also I react strongly against the male trait that is too proud to ask. I am happy to ask: I want to know; the men are usually pleased to tell me. My pride is not involved. If anything, I am proud of my humility in not minding. But then these psychological matters are rarely a single brash colour: they are mingled, subtle, like the plumage of a bird. Is there perhaps an inbuilt or programmed lack of confidence that dare not know things, that thinks, with knowledge comes responsibility, and I am afraid of that? I have come a long way from Standlake Common and the ducks, but it was the ducks that carried me. Watching Kate Humble on *Autumnwatch*, even the lovely and celebrated Kate Humble (though some believe that name is destiny), I notice that she deferred often to her male colleague, and even took the part of the wide-eyed disciple. I do not know to what extent she must follow a script, but surely, surely, these days young women are allowed to know things? But then I see how the disabling high heels we thought we'd binned for good are suddenly back, even higher. And recently the models on the fashion page appeared to be wearing nappies…

It is time to move to the second hide. I have eaten my lunch and made my list, which includes, besides all the seasonally-arrived ducks, a couple of the weirdly prehistoric-looking cormorants, with their wings spread like black washing, and one or two great-crested grebes, and coots and the shyer moorhens keeping to the reedy edges, and a heron, with its always-elderly look. I walk the third of a mile as fast as I can, to warm up.

Since I came last to this second hide someone has made a little structure from a dead branch and a pile of stones, presumably with the idea that it might make an attractive perch – perhaps for a kingfisher. Today though there is a persistent blue-and-orange absence, the same as with blue sky and sun, which was forecast, but never came. I find I am content – cold, but content. If all the days were halcyon days I would probably find them less precious. Like jewels, they need a setting. I watch a mute swan with arched wings sail after another, but whether in rivalry or with sexual intent I can't tell. I add a couple of gull species to my list. A single lapwing flying over is all the waders for the day.

I tend to favour what I think of as natural colours over the loud productions of a lab. But going back along the lane in a greyish light I am struck once again by the defiantly lurid liquorice all-sort pink of the spindle-berries, revealing the inner seeds as an equally garish, clashing orange. Even the leaves are the same kids'-crayon colour, in their autumn phase. No wonder that spindle was sometimes reckoned a witch-plant; it has all the lippy brightness of an ageing beauty; it won't give in to November.

At the end of the lane are still the electricity men in hard hats, like Bob the Builders placed there by a child from the Mulberry Bush School and then forgotten, still in a circle of three watching one who is up a pole. Perhaps they too need time to stand and stare. At the bus stop I watch another man wielding a little powered blower, blowing leaves from one place to another. It's the outdoor equivalent of a feather duster, equally inexplicable. Can anyone tell me why dust is better in my lungs than harmlessly lying still along the tops of books and pictures? And what an undignified end for feathers, domesticated and dyed pink. While I am waiting I observe a small patch of blue sky, the first and last of the day.

OT MOOR

After a record wet November, finishing with bad floods in Cumbria, the first day of December brought sunshine and the first frost of the year. My friend Diana, who lives in Oxford, has kept saying: "Let me know when there's been a frost and I'll come out and pick sloes"; but it didn't happen. It's probably too late now for the sloe gin to be ready for Christmas.

I ate porridge, dressed in five layers, made a sandwich, and walked across to the station, with the active tits and finches in the hedges seeming to enjoy the weather as much as I did. For the surprisingly small senior fare of £2.65 I got a ticket to Islip and back, my plan being to walk across the corner of Otmoor which is the RSPB reserve, and to take all day over it. There were fifty minutes to wait in Oxford for the Islip train, but I passed the time pleasantly with *The Guardian* crossword, and treated myself to a beaker of coffee that cost nearly as much as the ticket. It was a lot of years since I'd used the little station at Islip – so many that I wasn't sure if my memory of a coal fire in the waiting room was true or not.

The train travelled very slowly for some arcane railway reason, and I was able to relish the gradual loosening of Oxford's grip, and be received into the embrace of fields once more, but with the spice of their being less familiar than my own. There are black-headed gulls on the winter wheat in just the same way, and the river we cross is the same Cherwell I live by, only closer to where it finally, after many slow snakings, loses itself in the Isis. I catch sight of the Beckley wireless mast – that's where I'm headed, and it becomes my landmark, appearing and disappearing throughout the day, just as, in my childhood, my father would guide us through the Surrey countryside by repeated sightings of Leith Hill Tower. I also catch sight of a notice saying NO RIGHT OF WAY, and it comes to me that any such sign must indicate that there either is or at least was such a right, or that people have tried to pass that way because it looks like a pretty path or is a useful short cut. I wish I had more of the sort of courage shown by the poet Edward Thomas, who before he died for England at the end of the Great War, first walked and trespassed for it and urged the rest of us to do the same.

Islip station is on the outskirts of the village, and I am the only person getting on or off – one more than at Thomas's Adlestrop on that now famous occasion. I walk away once more between hedges full of birds. A golden fall of crab apples still lies on the frosty ground. Once in the village I pass with some trepidation the residence of Maddy and Beano who will "protect the gate" we are told if we step out of line. I'm still holding my urban takeaway coffee, symbol of the wired and pacey life I don't live, but a treat on a cold day. Islip too offers sustenance though. At the Red Lion the plastic Father Christmases are out already, and the little Swan, down by the River Ray, has a board out saying you can get hand-carved ham, egg, chips and a cup of tea or coffee for only £3. What with that and the train fare, I feel I'm in a time warp. I pass it with great regret, but I've got my lunch with me and anyway it's only half past eleven. But I'll definitely be back.

After crossing the River Ray my path leaves the road between allotments, and I am able to enjoy that mixture of admiration and envy that comes at the sight of other people's achievements in the matter of cabbages, parsnips and leeks. The Englishness of winter allotments overwhelms me with gratitude. I love it all – the damp huts, the dungheaps, the still-flowering marigolds, the half-stripped sprout rows, the evidence of patient, orderly, skilful, seasonal labour to cultivate the soil and get it to yield its fruits in this particular place. The endeavour, on these rented plots, seems to embody right livelihood and human-sized, unhubristic work to match our temporary tenancy of the earth.

The stile out into the fields is a little high for my stiffening skeleton, and I have to resort to a "One, Two, Three, HUP!" to get myself onto it. Well, I plan to go on walking for a good few years yet, and if in due course I have to wriggle under the bar like a dog in such situations, so be it. The path is now part of the Oxfordshire Way, a route using public rights of way across the county from Cotswolds to Chilterns. But long before that, the guide book to the long distance path tells me, this stretch was a coffin path, along which those people of Noke who paid their tithes to Islip were carried to their graves. This may explain the "metalling" of stone that shows under the thin mud line through the crops. It seems unlikely that they wrestled the tenanted coffins over stiles or through kissing gates though, so there must once have been wider ones or none at all. To me there is something very appealing about the idea of thus traversing one final time the quiet fields where one once walked.

But this morning I am very much alive, if a little creaky, in the calm, slightly misty sunshine, and receive a sudden thrill that lifts my spirits still higher at the sight of a red kite circling slow over the field, and then letting its long legs down, in a manner equally deliberate, and settling on the winter wheat. These birds are hard to miss now in the Chilterns, after their successful reintroduction some years ago, and they are spreading out; but in this part of the county they still cause us to look and exclaim. And next minute, as I pass through one of the round metal gates and glance to my left down the field, another bolt of excitement – there is a deer close to the hedge, stock still and staring back at me. I look through my binoculars to see it better, and admire the black borders to its ears. Then I realise there is a second animal behind the first, but it is an onlooker merely: it is the first I have to relate to. I lower the glasses, and we stay some time thus eye-locked. I have the distinct feeling it's more like the children's game of Who'll Blink First? than a tense poised moment of fear. I feel I am probably the more tense of the two of us. This is confirmed by the fact that when I eventually shift and it turns its heart-shaped white arse on me, it performs a couple of wildly exaggerated leaps and only moves a few yards.

Something makes me look back, as I walk away from the gate, and see a notice on it that I nearly missed. On the whole I am not a great fan of notices, especially in the countryside; but this one is different. It informs us that these fields are farmed in accordance with the principles of LEAF – Linking Environment and Farming – and explains a little about the crops and their uses, and the methods used of growing them without the over-use of chemicals. The language, the typography and the little drawings are all clear and simple and delightful. A child might take in this notice, and I observe with pleasure that there are in fact child-sized bootprints among those on the path. At the same time as informing this inspires and gives hope. All too recently the field next to where I live used to be sprayed from a tractor by a masked and white-suited operative straight out of a disaster movie, with fluid from a canister with a skull-and-crossbones on. I still remember the look of horror on his face – I saw it from my window – when, bending forward to make some adjustment, he felt a cold drip from the idle spraying arm on the unprotected back of his neck. That field has a footpath in it; it is our link to the main village. Even more disturbingly, someone or something is destined to eat what was grown there. Come to think of it, the guy's suit was identical with one I took out to India acting as courier for my journalist son-in-law, who was being sent to Iraq. Thankfully, he never needed to use it…

At the highest point in the field the roofs of Noke below can just be seen, and there is the Beckley mast once again. The path leads through a little group of thorns and small trees, and out onto the village road, where winter violets are flowering in the garden of Pixie Close. Pixie Close probably has nothing to do with garden gnomes: Pixie is from the same root as Pucksy, and Puck is an ancient, untameable, anarchic god of rural places. He crops up all over the south of England, and further afield too. The other houses have good rural names too – Nettles, The Plough, Stone Rise, Willow Tree House – and Puck belongs with them. Boggy and miry places are particularly to his liking, so with the whole moist moor ahead he might well hang out near here.

His is not the only supernatural power around though, even if it is the oldest: ahead on a miniature green where the cul-de-sac lane divides is the small, solid, ancient church – c.1270 we are told, and dedicated to

St.Giles. Somewhat unusually, and pleasingly to my eye, the bells hang visible in a separate bell cote. I walk on past and almost at once turn back. Some churches I can take or leave, but there is something about this one – its lack of consequence perhaps, its humility. It won't be open, of course. I try the door. It is open. I unlace my boots and leave them on the porch and go in. I'm pretty ignorant about church architecture and furnishings but, like the proverbial art philistine, I know what I like. I pad up the grass-green carpet and take a pew for a while. One side of the chancel arch is out of true, and the whole thing appears to lean a little crazily to one side, as a very old person is sometimes liable to do. An ever-green advent wreath with red candles hangs overhead. At the back of the church the little organ pipes are prettily painted with flowers in an arts-and-crafts kind of way. I like it here. There is nothing that feels churchy, only old, and deeply peaceful.

But the moor is calling. On the table the booklet requests that you not take it away, and offers instead a web address which I copy down grate-fully, liking the unfussy transition and continuity between the thirteenth and the twenty-first centuries. When I get home I look it up, and find one of the simplest and most beautifully designed websites I have come across, the pages set against a background of midnight blue. I learn that Giles, at one time apparently a very popular saint, was a hermit; and his emblematic animal (which I must not think of as a familiar) was a hind. Of course, had to be. That was what I saw on my way over – the one slightly in the background. The idea of a popular hermit intrigues me. Today footballers and models and so on are popular: but hermits? How can a recluse achieve popularity? It requires some mindset we've lost alto-gether. How long have we lived in the Age of Extraversion?

Booted once more I walk through the lower end of Noke where the houses overlook a quiet pasture with two piebald horses. Behind the houses a dozen black sheep are gathered round the common table of a hay feeder. A young man swoops past on a bike and calls "Hiya!" and I reply and feel blessed. I don't think he mistakes me for someone else: my brimmed hat and binoculars mark me out as a stranger. No, he is just friendly, and is glad that I am going to look at the birds and am enjoying the winter sunshine. An old rhyme says: "I went to Noke and nobody spoke – I went to Beckley, they spoke direckly". We shall see.

A jackdaw speaks too: "Jack! Jack!" from the roof of the manor house. Wild parsnips are still in flower along the ditch, and at the far end of Noke is a small bulrushy pond. I believe they are properly called reed-mace, but I grew up calling them bulrushes, and probably most people know what I mean. A tree that is bare of leaves but still hung with bright red apples looks like an arty piece of Christmas decoration. The eye delights in red in December – not so much in the high street, where it can become wearisome – but in the countryside where it warms the inner being as fire does the outer.

And as if on cue, as I turn out of the village, past a farm where they sell eggs and out onto the moor, I can see down ahead of me a couple of guys in orange jackets clearing scrub and stoking a fire with a flowing plume of blue smoke. A small stout vehicle, a kind of squat motorbike with a short trailer, comes towards me up the track, and the rider salutes me in friendly fashion as I step aside. It has cracked the thick ice on the puddles into pointed shards. A second farm, on my right, has house sparrows under its eaves; and I decide (after all there are no rules except of my own making) that my birdlist can start from now. This is the last house at this edge of the moor, and I don't expect to see sparrows again till I get to Beckley. And I am pleased to see them here. They used to be abundant round my house, which is similarly a last house; but now it is a matter of excitement to see a single one. Now if I ever hear that coarse chirping I rush to the window, and relish the sight of the actually very interestingly variegated chestnut and charcoal and mushroom plumage I used to think of as grey. So Here Beginneth my list, my lovely litany of the day's birds. Because I realise suddenly that it fulfils some such liturgical function for me: in naming it records, celebrates and cherishes. I'm not a professional ornithologist, and my list is no more practical than a prayer is, but it satisfies some of the same needs in me. Here is part of the answer to a problem that's bugged me since I lost my belief in God: what can be done with the instinct to pray? These last nine words were a line in one of my poems from that time, and I had no answers then. Maybe it helps to create a personal liturgy out of everyday life. Liturgy is only part of prayer though, and that inward inarticulate conversation still seems one-sided. Perhaps the answer will come to me as I continue my mini-pilgrimages.

Meanwhile I have erred and strayed too far from the earth, always a mistake in spiritual matters in my opinion, and I'm not even out to write a spiritual book. It takes a harmless revenge as with my head in the clouds I step incautiously into an ice-broken rut and slop freezing, muddy water over the top of one of my boots. In a thin stretch of hedge, on my right, a small shapely sallow with just a few leaves remaining shows its structure: it is shaped like a candle flame. On my left, the entire, wide, water-filled ditch is frozen solid. A single beehive sits on the broad verge, under the hedge, which soon becomes tall and overgrown, and punctuated with scions of the old oaks that gave Noke its name, when it was a clearing in the forest at the fen's edge. Today they are full of winter thrushes, which I seem unintentionally to be herding ahead of me as one sometimes does with sheep that have strayed into a green lane. I notice once again how deceptive can be the size of birds in silhouette.

At the next junction of lanes I realise what's going on. I'd heard that the RSPB had acquired a little more land and planned a hide, and here it is, almost built. Those guys were probably involved in the carefully planned management of the wetland for the benefit of birds. There is no access yet to the hide, though I can smell the new timber a hundred yards away, and no birds on the new scrapes at present – I imagine because of all the human activity. I can see yet another fire beyond it. Then I realise that a couple of people are standing still away to my left, near the bend in the path by the first screen. A few minutes earlier I'd glanced round and seen no-one and had a pee – all that coffee! Could they have seen me? Peeing is a tricky on Otmoor because there's little cover and everyone has binoculars. But what – apart from me – were they watching? In very early spring this year there had been a bittern for a spell, and it hung out in just that area, providing a kind of one-bird show as it teased us by vanishing and then reappearing and stalking about with an odd gait and even odder frozen attitudes, like someone involved in a game of musical statues.

That's the way I am headed, so there's nothing for it but to brazen it out. In any case, if there is a bittern, or anything else exciting, I want to see it. This next track, which forms part of the "visitor trail", has a bank to one side which you are asked not to climb. It's frustrating not to view the wide levels beyond, but there are other places from which to see them, and good birders' reasons for keeping one's head down here. Another is the wind that often blows and receives no check from anything else in the landscape. As I come level with the two people I can see that they are two fence-mending guys who haven't even got binoculars, and who are stationary because they are blamelessly eating their lunch. They show no sign of having seen me, now or earlier, and the sight of their munching speeds me round the corner, up the slope and onto the bench inside the viewing screens. The water ahead of me through the window in the wattled fencing is full of ducks. Mostly they are folded and floating, in siesta. There are a few flutters and splashes, and a quiet background noise of wigeon squeals and muted quacking. That must be the tower of the church of Charlton-on-Otmoor in the distance opposite. In the foreground are gold-lit, rounded stands of reed, and above them big soft sweepings of cloud.

After a while a party of half a dozen birders arrives and I set off for the second screen, half a mile on. Another lone watcher has also jumped ship a little ahead of me, and I hear part of his conversation with one coming in the opposite direction: "…a couple of Cetti's, you can hear them but you don't see them!" I know where he means: I too have heard but not seen, on earlier visits.

Ahead and to the left must be Oddington church. I experience a touch of my litanising urge: I want all seven "towns", as they were known, to be counted, invoked, protected: Beckley, Noke, Oddington, Charlton, Fencott, Murcott, Horton-cum-Studley.

A huge, flame-coloured crop of fungi has erupted out of a damp tree-stump. To my left two more Noke oaks stand in a green field in that particularly English and steadying way. I catch up with the man ahead, and he asks me about ducks. "I never remember which are wigeon and which are teal," he says, and I explain as well as I can, though unscientifically, flustered and a little pleased to find, for a change, a man who knows less than I do. As we approach the screen bullfinches fly circumspectly up the hedge ahead of us, but he can never see them. It reminds me of watching a meteor shower once with a few friends, and us all calling out every few minutes "Look! There's one! Over there! There's another!" but one of the party ruefully somehow was always focused elsewhere. Right by the screen is a treeful of cormorants, sitting still and looking old, or cold and, as to my eye they always do, rather uncomfortable in their skins. They take no notice of us at all.

The other guy goes, and I finish my lunch alone watching this new stretch of water. A largish raptor makes a brief, low flight. I wonder if it is a harrier, but a new birder arrives, and asks, as you do, "Anything about?", which means anything of interest, and I tell him, and he thinks it is a buzzard known to be in the area which, he says placatingly, can act just like a harrier, quartering the fen. He is the usual kind of birder, who obviously knows much more than I do, and he convinces me. But he is an aesthete too, no mere gruff male twitcher. "Lovely, isn't it?" he enthuses, of the day and the scene, even though there's "not much about" of real birding note, "Absolutely beautiful!" I like a man who can see and say that.

On my way back I catch sight of a single snipe flying high and fast, and there are small flocks of gulls and of lapwings. At the corner by the screen once more, this time I rapturously breathe in an aromatic plant smell which I missed on the way out. I am glad to find it still in place. Every time I visit Otmoor, summer or winter, I smell it, and I'm always asking, if anyone else is about to ask, if they know what it is. Most people sniff and say: "Oh, yes! So there is!" But no-one so far has volunteered to identify it. There's a tangle of vegetation growing in or near the water just there, and a fence, so it can't be investigated thoroughly. My best guess is bog myrtle, also known as sweet gale, which is a small aromatic shrub "locally common" my plant book says "in fens and bogs throughout most of Britain".

Halfway along the next track is where the Cetti's warblers live, and they do actually live, all the year round, unlike most warblers, which are summer visitors. I'm listening hard. Not that you have to listen hard for the song, which is a little loud melodic explosion more likely to make you jump. They do it much less in winter, but they can sing on any bright day. Something calls – calls rather than sings – low down among the stalks, and I pause to try to see it. There's something small and brown on the move, always half-hidden. I seem to get a glimpse of grey as well, and wonder about a dunnock. Then I see the upturned tail. Oh! It must be a wren. It makes a few unwrenlike sounds, chip, chip. The tail too is not quite right. OK, it's upturned, but it's very broad. And the whole bird seems slightly larger and slightly more solid than a wren. Then it flies across the path and from the swift and slightly twisty way it drops down into the reeds I know it isn't a wren. Then I realise: it's a Cetti's! I've actually seen one! Where are the birders when you want them? But ten to one if I hadn't been alone I wouldn't have seen it. I check the book when I get home, still half-expecting to have been wrong, but no – Cetti's – it has to be. So often I've heard the song in just that place. All's far from right with the world in so many ways, the lark in particular often not being on the wing as in *Pippa Passes*, but, just for a moment there, everything was.

It's beginning to cloud over and maybe even to dusk a little, towards three in the afternoon, with the shortest day only three weeks off. A swan here and there in the grass or on the water shows up well, but it's getting harder to see the other birds. When I reach the feeders there's a squirrel plastered upside down against one of them, and it's still there, eating as though for a contest, when I leave ten minutes later. Tits and finches come and go on the other two. A great spotted woodpecker takes off from the nearby trees and heads for the belt on the far side, and a moment later is followed by a second. Their unevenly bounding flight make them a clumsy-looking pair, and I smile – they make me think of me and Jeremy trying to dance in the kitchen and not quite meshing.

Small red lights are showing on the Beckley mast. High up where it is still light are soft silver puffs of cloud and below them darker grey ones looking more solid. Hamlet – or Tolkien – would have noticed that they look like dragons. Big chunky red necklaces of bryony hang in the hedge, and then I catch sight, further up Otmoor Lane, of a woman in a seasonal bright red fleece walking home with her dog. The lane keeps on going uphill to where Beckley sits on the edge as if ready to repel all boarders, so I sit gratefully for a while on a millennium bench halfway up to gaze at the view. By now the clouds are lit with a peachy glow. Three or four horses in blankets are grazing quietly. The moor stretches away into the distance, its hedges merging to give the appearance of a wood. I can see Smokey Joe, the old cement works chimney close to where I live. If I could summon a dragon cloud I'd be home in no time.

In the village I sit on another seat opposite the pub and start to wait for the bus and, true to the rhyme, a friendly native immediately plies me with talk. She knows nothing of any bus. She seems to regard them as a slightly suspicious and new-fangled invention. After she's gone the door of the pub opens and someone comes out for a smoke. "Are they open in there?" I call. "We're putting up the Christmas decorations," she says. "Come and sit by the fire." So once more I leave my boots in a porch and enter an open house, and this time I sip red wine too, and watch the logs burn with their timeless comfort, until the bus comes cheerfully out of the dark and takes me back to Oxford, and the train home.

CHURN KNOB

The path across the field behind the house felt harder than a metalled road, perhaps in contrast to its normal yieldingness. Every stalk was a white cactus. The ground itself and the trees were thickly coated with frost. As I waited for the bus the sky was clear blue and the sun shone on the gold-tipped weathervane and clock-face of the church. Out of sight but somewhere close by starlings were conversing.

This New Year excursion is a bid for freedom – mostly from sludgy bits of myself. It's a stepping out into and laying hold on the future, a reclaiming of my life after a really crap Christmas. My friend Simon's Dad talks to me on the bus – they had a bad Christmas too with several people ill.

"You are blessed with a sanguine temper," a kindly but pontifical old Welsh poet once told me, and I agree. I think I am fundamentally optimistic. Every year I look forward to Christmas, even though that festival has sometimes turned out to be anything but jolly. And here I am again, heading for the hills, hopeful that this year will go well, hopeful of having a happy day today. I've been to "workshops" where you are invited to change chairs in order to get a new perspective on things, with the object of facing your demons or tracking down your angels. And it does help:

a very small move can show you a whole different view. And a whole day out in different surroundings can bring about a quite dramatic change of mood or even of mind.

I'm lucky enough to live in what many people would see as itself an oasis – in fact many friends have experienced it as such. But the elements of pilgrimage, the effort involved in getting to one's destination, and the sense of aiming somewhere special and desirable, these are altogether different from simply staying at home, however pleasant home is. Home waits for your return, and that too is a pleasure, as the agreeably weary and spiritually recharged you re-encounters its familiarity, puts a match to the stove, starts peeling the spuds.

It's bitterly cold, despite the sun, and I'm wearing my magically warm but totally un-p.c. fur hat. I excuse it to myself and others by telling how I bought it at my friend Jeanie's jumble sale, when she was moving house, and how she had acquired it years before in Afghanistan where she grew up. I don't even know what kind of fur it is, but it's soft and beautiful, variegated whitey-brown, and no "fleece" or even wool or felt hat comes close to it for warmth. Perhaps it has some kind of shamanic effect, because I feel invigorated when I am wearing it – bright-eyed and bushy-tailed one might say – and people respond to me differently from usual. As yet not many days in England call for it, but this is one of them, and so added to my pleasure in playing hooky from my everyday life is that of being properly equipped and comfortable.

I run through my upper garments in my head and realise I'm wearing six layers, with two on my legs and three on my feet. Also, I have a wooden stick, which gives me huge confidence on hard and slippery ground. It balances me physically, but there's a psychological element too. I can understand why the mage-writer John Cowper Powys was inseparable from his and even gave it a name.

In Oxford I change buses, and soon we are shooting out across the shining Thames, through Grandpont, past a flock of Canada geese grazing on frozen grass, past Cow Mead allotments, past Fat Phil's Angling Centre and the boarded-up Fox and Hounds. There's a sinister-looking person on the bus's CCTV, swaddled and squat. I look round anxiously for this loony or terrorist, and then realise it's – surely distorted? – me.

The Orchard Centre in Didcot is all shops and roads and concrete. I feel a little sad for the fruit trees that were once there, but I'm soon on the move again, weaving through villages, and then as we come into Blewbury on my feet and asking for the Load of Mischief. The driver says, yes, not far, and then forgets to tell me. Sadly, because a pub of that name sounds a lively place, it has closed down, so I don't see it myself. He pulls up suddenly and embarassedly when he remembers, and gives garbled directions. The pavements are terrifyingly slippery and I proceed with extreme slowness, already thankful for my pilgrim's staff.

By now I have the map out and my glasses, and am trying to figure out exactly where in this quite sizeable village I am. A native who is just preparing to venture out in his 4x4 is friendly, and gentlemanly. He first of all explains where I am, and then says that since he is driving past the ends of the bridleways that lead up to Churn Knob, why doesn't he give me a lift. He chooses the one that he reckons will be the easiest going, and with good wishes on his side and grateful thanks on mine we part company, and I commence the central stage of my quest.

As at home, the rutted mud is frozen rock-hard, and so actually the going is relatively easy compared with the pavements, up the narrow, steep, ancient track between thorn bushes. There are plenty of violets leaves – there will be flowers in a few weeks – and I imagine that in summer there will be flowers of all kinds beneath the thorns. All that there is today by way of colour are some highly distinctive plants with orange berries in split-apart brown pods. The leaves are speary, like montbretia. When I look them up back at home they seem to be *iris foetidissima*, stinking iris, also known as gladdon, or roast-beef plant, growing on chalk in a south country hedge-bank, just as it should. *Flora Britannica* suggests the smell has been over-stated, and says it is sometimes grown in churchyards for the colour it provides when no other is available. There are not many birds about either – rooks and winter thrushes – but not many small birds.

The path takes me round the edge of a vast disused chalk pit, and by the time I reach the seat placed above it on the turf I'm a little out of breath and warm enough to sit down, untie the hat's Davy Crockett tails from under my chin to let them hang down, and relish a view and a sandwich. The prospect is back towards Didcot with its chimneys, but set in a wide sweep of pasture and arable land. This area was until fairly recently part of Berkshire. Reorganisation meant that a small part of the classic downland landscape with its special geology, prehistory and wildlife is now ours to call our own in Oxfordshire – though it does still feel a bit like stealing.

Two women suddenly appear up the track coming fast, perhaps in their lunch hour. They are smiling and breathless as they sit down with me on the seat. I ask them how much further it is, and in what exact direction, to Churn Knob, and they look nonplussed, waving vaguely in what turns out later to be not quite the right direction. After a while they go back down, but I am not alone for long – a vision out of Greek mythology appears – a man sitting under a coloured sail and borne aloft like Icarus. He appears to be holding on hard with both hands. I wave, and immediately wish I hadn't, in case he waves back and falls out of the sky.

Continuing up the hill I emerge at a crossing of tracks onto a field of inch-high brassicas. I can see a pole on a tump in the middle of it, but no clump of hawthorns, such as I have seen in pictures of the Knob. A large bird of prey vanishes behind it too quickly for me to note points to identify it. I choose one track and then leave it for another, where there is a small coppice. Maybe that's what I am looking for. But when I get there a notice warns people off, and so I decide to follow a different bridleway down, past what the map marks as access land, and which the two women had referred to as "the nature wood". When I reach the wood there seems to be no way in, but a gate leads into a pasture above it, so steep that it's hard to stay upright while walking along the contour. I walk right round to the bottom of the wood but there is no way in through the fencing, although the women had warned me to be careful of fallen trees, and there inside the fence, some fallen trees are, and notices tell us to be careful of ground-nesting birds. You can see into the wood well enough from this vantage point, and in summer perhaps could even sit here and watch. The steep pasture appears to be full of ancient molehills, but something I read later suggests to me that maybe these aren't mole-hills but anthills – maybe sitting here wouldn't be such a good idea. I once got an ant-bite that took a month to heal.

I make my way back to the track and slowly down, but once down I still feel frustrated, and gaze back up, unwilling to give up. And as often happens to a woman at a loss, a man comes by and offers his help. This one really wants to help, it isn't the landowner's plummy and contemptuous "Can I help you?" which means just the opposite.

When I explain my dilemma, how I've been up already but failed to locate the "Knob", he leaps up the path at speed, his Alsatian well-behaved (normally I would be terrified) because I am under his protection. I've never been much good at hills, although I have reasonably good stamina, and can go a long way, on the flat. Soon I have to pant that I'm sorry, and don't let me hold him up, but I can't go this fast… Imagine my shame when he apologises and slows down, and soon after tells me that he is seventy-five! I can give him ten years. I pull my hat right off because by now I'm overheated, and seeing my grey hair he realises I'm a pensioner too. Perhaps he was showing off for what he thought was a younger woman, but he still has to be amazingly fit. I ask again about the Knob, and he waves at the chalk pit where I had lunch and tells me how it provided material for the old cob houses and walls for which Blewbury is famous. He seems to want me to shift my interest to something else, something more canny. He tells me how he has lived in the village all his life and his father and grandfather before him. He tells me how he loves the place, and again waves his hand, this time over the whole wide view, saying: "It's free! All this, and it's free!"

"What," he asks, "would I want with going on holiday, when I have all this?" His lively contentment feels like a rare and very precious thing. Perhaps it accounts for what seems a Puck-like sprightliness, a rude health, an abundance of animal spirits. And he doesn't even have a fur hat…

He questions me. I murmur about being a mother and a housewife, and finally am driven by something in him to candour, and admit that I scribble a bit. I tell him I love walking and exploring, and that I'm writing about that. "And the funny people you meet," he adds shrewdly, and grinning like the hobgoblin I half think he is.

I press him again about the Knob. If anyone knows, he does. And strangely, he comes over sheepish. "I feel such an idiot, such an idiot," he keeps repeating. "Do you know, all these years, and I've never been there?" He points me out the way though: it is the now treeless tump that I saw before, enisled in an inch-high crop, with no path for the last hundred yards. "You won't do much harm, at this time of year," he throws over his shoulder, departing in his rapid and magical way. Clearly I have to do this last leg alone.

I lurk furtively across. The ancient thorn trees and grass have indeed gone, and the mound, the mound itself, is covered weirdly with flat chicken wire, not as fencing, but flat against the earth. Stuck upright in the tump is a short length of scaffolding pole with a metal star of David stuck on top – a puzzling and unattractive decoration made worse by the senseless graffiti scrawled on it. A huge and heavy wooden cross, twice my height, lies on the ground. It's an odd place.

Back at home I look into it some more on the web. Apparently a few years back some kind of controversy took place when the then vicar wanted to erect a cross on the prehistoric barrow to remember the beginning of the preaching mission of one St. Birinius, and from what I saw it looked as though it was still unresolved. He reckoned he had the necessary permission: others disagreed. Some said the cross had been erected in the wrong place, meaning, the wrong place by a matter of yards. Others said it was wrong in the sense of being unsuitable altogether. Pagan websites said a beautiful and sacred place had been violated, and was it now therefore open season for plastering pagan symbols on Christian churches? Whoever dreamed up the scaffolding thing wasn't (in my opinion) helping.

The view now extended even further round, from this high point, across the almost non-existent hamlet of Churn, famous as a birding spot, and mile on mile of sparsely-inhabited farmland criss-crossed by hedges and beginning now to be misty.

Taking over pagan sites and superimposing the new religion on them was, as I understand it, the usual strategy. Birinius was on message. This particular cross has a distinct air of defeat, lying there gigantic and slain on the mud, but after all Christianity (if I understood it right) was at least as much about defeat as it was about triumph. Personally, I would cart it away – it would keep our wood-burner going a good week – and the scaff pole and the mysterious chicken wire – and set a few slips of hawthorn, and ask forgiveness of whatever supernatural powers take an interest for our clumsy human messings about. For, despite everything, the place felt numinous.

Some months later I was again in Blewbury, and the spring flowers were out. Jeremy and I were en route to a gig in Basingstoke, and I still had some questions. We wandered round its tight little warren of picturesque streets and admired the famous cob walls with doors that looked meant for hobbits. I ventured into the church and asked a lady who was tidying up after a Sunday service what she could tell me about the deposed cross. As I was coming to expect, her face clouded over. "I can't get up there, with this leg," she murmured. It sounded like an excuse: I didn't get the impression she had ever been up there, even pre-arthritis. "Thrown down, is it?" she ponders sadly, "I must tell the new vicar..." And she commences to recount how improbably many clubs and societies Blewbury has, as a way to raise it once more in my estimation.

We then walked up Blewbury's other hill, Blewburton Hill, which is approached by a concrete path past a ripe farmyard, and which was over-flown, when we saw it, by six or seven red kites. This too is an ancient site. It is a far more substantial earthwork: an entire iron age hill fort, though less high than Churn Knob. Legend and archaeology have their usual inconclusive stories to tell about it. Legend does not pretend to do more than mirror our nightmares or our dreams; and I confess to being sceptical about archaeologists' pronouncements, despite (or perhaps because of) having been brush-and-dustpan girl on a Roman site one school holidays, and later trailing hot and dusty in the wake of my ex-husband round ancient Greek sites, trying in vain to visualise "the throne room", "the store-room" or "a place set aside for ritual purposes". I also remember reading the arguments about Troy. I loved the bit in Rose Macaulay's *The Towers of Trebizond* where someone declaims Virgil *iam seges sunt ubi Trioa fuit* and someone else matter-of-factly counters, "Well, hardly *seges*, just grass and things."

There's plenty of grass here, and an enclosed and car-free space, but Churn Knob is higher and windier and probably more ancient, and despite what seems to be almost a local phobia about going there, and despite the unfinished religious war, I preferred it. You never know what you might meet. I made Jeremy walk with me again up that one too, and then that night in Basingstoke Darren Black was singing, and I caught the words "refuge of the tired and ragged souls". Yeah, that's it, and it will not, as the cryptic crossword setters have it, be further defined.

ABINGDON MUSEUM

Sometimes the past is the peace you hanker for. Especially just before spring kicks in. Not the real past, with its rank breath and lack of sanitation, its mud and blood and frightful surgery, and its incomprehensible coarseness – so very different in feel from our twenty-first century coarseness – but the dusty, crumbling past of museums. The only trouble is that the rage for cleaning and tidying and displaying and explaining things to within an inch of their lives makes this kind of peace hard to come by nowadays. Call me perverse, but I like old-style local museums where they jumbled things a little, when a flint axe, a stuffed bird, a meteorite and a child's worm-eaten wooden cradle all shared the space, when labels were hand-written on slips of yellowing card, where you peered at the exhibits as though they were from another world. That way, one's imagination had a little room to breathe, and the things were allowed the dignity of dying. Literature is full of the horrors of everlasting life; think of Butler's *Erewhon* or Wilde's Dorian Gray. And my Moscow-based daughter Phoebe tells me they are even thinking of letting Lenin have a decent burial.

Edward Thomas wrote in praise of the dust on nettles, sweetly, as he did about so many neglected things; and I am a lover of dust also, in its place, which is underfoot, or in an old house. I do not feel at ease in a house that is too clean. I haven't visited the famously smelly museum in York, not because I'm squeamish about ordure, but because to my mind museums should smell of dust, and of the carbolic soap in their cold lavatories. Visiting my daughter when she was in India, I found several small museums of the old sort, that ought to be in museums… No-one, not even the attendants, seemed to understand what was in them. I suppose no-one had touched them since the days of the Raj. They did not have displays that lit up by means of interactive buttons. Like almost everywhere in India except the Oberoi Hotel they had dust in abundance. But one can have too much of a good thing. When I once said to Phoebe, who was at that time Delhi-based, that I would rather buy my bathroom things somewhere a bit less seedy, she shrugged resignedly, and said: "These are the upmarket shops!"

On a hunch I decided to visit Abingdon Museum. Abingdon is on the far side of Oxford from me, and over my nearly fifty years of living in the county I'd hardly ever been there. And when I first arrived, it wasn't even in the county, but, like Churn, in Berkshire. The Ashmolean has recently reopened after its two-year mega-springclean, though it always seemed pretty tidy to me already. Over the years I'd got to know where my favourite things were, and once even was allowed to organise a small exhibition in there, of the English paintings and drawings from their collection which featured footpaths. Going through stacks of beautiful things not usually on view wearing special gloves was a huge treat. But a few days ago I put my ill-advised head inside and left after five minutes feeling rather sick. Too many people and too few walls suddenly. I shall make myself go back when the excitement has died down, and maybe I shall get used to it eventually. My friend Lynn writes from London that she would like to come and see the Eastern art: that will be a good way in – she will help me to look. In the meantime I suddenly wondered if Abingdon had escaped the makeover madness.

I asked the bus driver to tell me which stop was nearest to the Town Hall, and he kindly turned round and asked the bus. A good omen! Someone owned up to knowing, and I walked pretty well straight off the bus and in, and up the stairs, eager, after my journey, for the loo. The fact that there wasn't one, and that I was advised to go to the Guildhall, and that the Guildhall to which I hastily repaired turned out to be shut on a Monday, whereupon I threw myself on the local knowledge of two young women with pushchairs who were stood in the street sorting the world out, and one of whom said she must be on her way anyway, and if I came with her to the Baptist Hall where there was a playgroup, which was where she was headed, she was certain they'd be fine about me going in "for a wee", which they were – all this only added in my eyes to the Museum's charm, to my sense that I might have struck gold.

Back at the Town Hall once more, a fine building dating from the late sixteenth century, one of those market buildings with an upper room standing above a pillared area below, I was able to enjoy the stairwell properly. It was satisfyingly draughty; and the thick wooden banisters with huge round bobbles (for which there is no doubt a proper architectural term) at each turn were painted an indescribably non-modern colour. I couldn't decide if it was grey, blue or green. Perfect! Ascending slowly and paying attention to the little wall cases, I was taken on an agreeable short journey through the centuries of Abingdon, beginning with a selection of tiny sharp flint tools that made me suddenly aware of the beauty and variety of flint as a substance. There was also an egg-shaped piece that looked as though it would fit comfortably in one's palm, and which sure enough was described as "an ovate hand-axe". Onwards and upwards, past decorated "Abingdon ware", past the Romans, the Anglo-Saxons, the monks, the guilds…

The current exhibition was of the art and artists of Abingdon, and the single exhibition room filled with very modern glass cases, trimmed with very blond wood, matching the large number of what I eventually identified as chairs. I was never quite sure if these chairs were exhibits, or whether one was allowed to sit on them. They looked so very clean and new that I didn't quite dare. They were also completely flat, and I had the feeling my bum would look big in them. Also I am not square. Reading up on them later in a book I bought, I discovered that they were famous and special, and that the money to pay for them had come from the sale of some older exhibition cases. Clutching my printed sheet, I circled the contemporary cases trying to match the numbers on them with that, and failing. I believe I am afflicted with some slight disorder akin to dyslexia, because I can rarely follow such things. It's the same with plans of gardens or nature reserves. In the end I give up, and just wander.

I am drawn to a smart, bold painting of a coach and four: "Francis Blewitt's coach: the Abingdon Machine. On its first journey from London. c.1767." The sky is blue and the clouds are white and birds are on the wing. The coachman has a whip, and a woman sits next to him. On top are two men and a woman, two men face backwards and a man and a woman sit inside. I am interested that not all the women sit inside: perhaps cost came into it. But whatever the truth of that, here is an adventure being embarked on! These people are all shaking their ideas up a little too, just as I am, as they bounce along, and they are making the journey, at any rate in this particular way, for the first time. The coach-maker is proud of his achievement. Today he would have taken a photograph; but then today we don't usually undertake horse-drawn travels.

In the corner of the frame is a small, dead spider, and all at once I begin to be more at home here. To be sure insects have a way of getting themselves behind picture-glass and perishing in the best-regulated estab-lishments, and it means little except annoyance to the house-proud. To me it is (paradoxically) a vital link restored. It speaks of the behovely passing of time, of the death and decay which despite our cheeriest, most housewifely instincts we cannot prevent. I've written elsewhere about my hankering for the days when second-hand bookshops were a little less hoovered and organised, and when pressed flowers, or old letters, might still occasionally be found inside the books. Junk shops too are not what they were. Mostly now their flotsam has received a lot of attention from chemical cleaners of various kinds, and the glory-holes aspire to be thought of as antique shops. For a while charity shops could still hit the spot; but most of these now have managers who clack up and down talking into mobile phones and who bully the hapless volunteers into something like professionalism. Probably they have targets, and business plans. I realise that they exist to make money for good causes, and not to nourish my soul. I merely remark that some excellent sources of soul food have now dried up, and one needs to search elsewhere.

Some of my happiest hours as a child were spent in the Natural History Museum in Kensington. I was allowed to travel in on the District Line from the suburbs at a much younger age than would be considered safe now. My favourite galleries were British Birds – turn left and go down to a circular room at the end where stuffed birds sat in pretend habitats behind glass, and Minerals, upstairs and on the right, where I could gaze at lavender or turquoise or gold pieces of glittering, encrusted rock. Jewellers' windows, where the gems are taken from their rocks and polished, did not hit the spot at all. This was well before the heyday of nature films, and in any case we had no telly. Then as now there is no substitute for the wild; but for one suburban child this was a way of furnishing the imagination with an idea of the strangeness and variety of nature.

Looking out of the window I can see Costa, Jessops, M & Co, Coffee Republic, Nat West and Lloyds TSB. And the colour and movement of a street market. From this window since this room held the Sessions, the market has been visible below, and probably the ancestors of these pigeons flying up in bevvies like leaves, as they are today. Despite internet "shopping", shopping malls and supermarkets, there's something enlivening about a street market that we haven't wanted to lose. It's cheering, and kind of surprising, that standing in a queue in all weathers, and being part of a lively crowd despite being slightly anxious about one's purse, is something we've wanted to hang on to, something that's considered not just tolerable but positively enjoyable.

The rise of the farmers' markets brought back to me my year in Washington D.C. in 1970-1. To my great relief, I had discovered the Montgomery Farm Women's Co-operative, on the outskirts, and I used to go each week, as much for a breath of fresh air as for a basket of fresh food. The women seemed almost to belong to a different race from their urban sisters. Their clothes and hair and speech were all different, and they wore no make-up. Like the W.I. over here, they also sold some home-cooked things very different from what you could get in Safeway. I hope they're still trucking.

But to wander back into the museum, they say now that too sanitised an environment may cause allergies, and that we need to encounter germs to build up our resistance. I wonder if the same is true for the spirit? It usually does seem that what is true for us physically has its counterpart in something psychological. So I'm hoping that maybe the new age of austerity will allow any small forgotten museums that have somehow got away to continue their gentle decline.

The more I expand on this, the more puzzled I become, because I do want old things honoured and shared; and moreover there is nothing intrinsically moral or uplifting about being cold while you look at them. I think perhaps in the end it is to do with discovery. Discovering things for oneself is always going to be more thrilling than admiring someone else's discoveries; and being thrilled, having one's imagination ignited, feeling a sense of the ineluctable weirdness of matter, is to be truly alive. Something in us needs a mystery – why else are detective stories so popular? More exaltedly, we need a sense of wonder, and if explanation can never remove that altogether, still it often seems to limit it in some way. It can become too clean, too quality-controlled. It's the same with supermarket veg, which comes chemically grown and preserved, without a speck of earth on it. And some of us are beginning to rebel, and demand it more natural again.

On the wall, permanently dislayed, is a mirror with a frame thought to be made by the famous wood-carver Grinling Gibbons. The pale lime-wood has darkened with the years, but is still light enough to contrast beautifully with the darker oak surround. I eagerly copy down a quota-tion from Horace Walpole:

There is no instance of a man before Gibbons who gave to wood the look and airy lightness of flowers, and chained together the products of the elements with a free disorder, natural to each species.

Since then I have happened on the same passage quoted in Richard Mabey's rich and strange cornucopia *Flora Britannica*. This is a book which I have only come to recently, with that slightly superstitious feeling of serendipity that it is just the right moment, that there was a reason why one held back until now. Be that as it may, I have been enjoying it like a wonderful herbal cordial, allowing myself an hour a day, to prolong the pleasure and sense of healthful benefit. The entry on Lime gives this same quotation which I need not apologise for airing once again, since it clearly must contain some kind of widely-acknowledged magic. There is certainly something in the way the words "free" and "natural" seed themselves in our minds that hints at a process as inexplicable as life itself mercifully still is. Walpole puts his finger on, or at least points out, something we want words for, but in doing so he merely celebrates, he does not explain it, least of all does he explain it away.

Moving on, I admire the Borough Measures, in solid brass with handles, Imperial Weights: Half Gallon, Gallon, Peck, Half Bushel. From a barrel-topped money chest I raise my eyes to the High Street banks, and rather wish my small stash was in one such as this, rather than, somewhat notionally, out there.

Wanting refreshment I pause by the coffee-machine, but quickly decide I won't be able to work it, and at the same time rather wanting a human hand to brew and hand me my cup, I clump once more down the long-suffering stairs and out into the street. Almost at once I encounter Local Roots, where everything has been made within thirty miles of Abingdon, and a slow, restorative cup of coffee can be enjoyed while you sit and take in a variety of hand-crafted things.

From there it is a wandering step or two down to the Thames, which is the major reason for Abingdon's long settlement and prosperity. Boats are moored up at St. Helen's Wharf, and I sit for a while enjoying the vigorous pre-spring quacking of the mallards as they paddle past going with the current, and therefore at some speed, on water lighted olive-green by a weeping willow, and the multi-layered pastel colours of the plane bark – eau-de-nil, ochre, cinnamon, grey – in little jigsaw-like shapes. The colours of old rooms. Everything seems very solid – the seat I am on, the black ornate posts and rails along the waterside, the attractively uneven old half-timbered houses with their jutting tops, the churchyard hollies and yes, the very gravestones. Someone is playing the organ.

I catch a whiff of that smell that lives inside old wooden recorders. I do not know what causes it, or where else it may live – I can see no recorders anywhere at hand – but it speaks to me of old wooden things, and of things laid by. Marcel Proust would have written twenty pages about it. Proust is someone else I've only just come to, but after the excitement of feeling I'd met something of a kindred spirit in the first volume, who allowed himself to ramble following his thoughts, and who took as long as it took, I ploughed miserably on through three or four more, hoping against hope that he would find his way again. Finally I tired completely of his ego and his voyeurism and returned him to the library (he was relegated to the stack for a good reason I reckoned) with disappointment and disgust. I reminded myself of a wonderfully liberating few words of Doris Lessing's in a preface to a new edition of *The Golden Notebook.* She encourages us to follow our liking in our reading, to ramble, to let one thing lead to another, and never to read anything that we are not drawn to because we feel we ought. It is a good principle for one's actual ramblings also.

Treasures are personal, little objects or sayings, the grace of a particular flower, are sometimes potent for oneself alone. Sometimes, like Walpole on Gibbons, the same thing will speak to many. But if, like the way pigeons fly in the wind, or the patterns on a plane tree, or a dead spider, they are more idiosyncratic, still they are almost certainly shared by some. I learn of course that Abingdon's museum is due for the treatment: I've only just got here in time.

PORT MEADOW

There's a painting in the Ashmolean that both my son Nat and I have been drawn to – *A Study in March* by John William Inchbold – to the extent that we use it as a shorthand way of referring to a particular kind of early spring day. There's a small clump of primroses in the foreground and what looks like cuckoo flower, a.k.a lady's smock; but what dominates the picture are the irregular shapes of old tree trunks, their bark shown in all its fractured detail. To me it is the netted beauty of the bare twigs against cold blue sky and the way the sun lights up one leaning trunk in particular that is the quintessence of early spring, with its slightly scary invitation to – as they say in the States – start over.

Goeffrey Grigson, in a lovely book called *Britain Observed*, dug out some lines of Swinburne's that celebrate Inchbold as a painter of light:

> *To thee the sun spake, and the morning sang*
> *Notes deep and clear as life…*

So today is an Inchbold day, and here I am waiting at the Green in Tackley for the Oxford bus on the first of March after a very long cold winter. There's still frost underfoot but the sun's out, and the sky as blue as the little scillas I noticed the other day in someone's lawn in St. John's Road. On our way in to town we pass two rookeries with plenty of action. By means of the bus lane we slide grandly ahead of the queue up the Banbury Road. I get off and walk through Jericho towards Port Meadow.

This trip is mildly counter-intuitive. Mainly I shun Oxford with its modern shops and crowds and the lordly weight of its history. Not that I am a Jude figure – they did let me in, and I studied at Somerville in the sixties – but I think I must have a rural soul. Besides which, I dislike whatever has an air of consequence. However, Port Meadow offers just the kind of oasis I am writing about – it has its own identity, is free from cars and free of charge. Besides which, I have my own history with the place.

When I and a curly-haired lad were a mere foolish twenty years old, in the second year of our studies, we got married. One result of this was that we were no longer obliged to live in university-approved lodgings, so we forthwith set up home in a couple of rooms in a house in Jericho which enjoyed the reputation of having been a brothel, although it seemed perfectly respectable when we were there. Most of the comings and goings were of our friends coming to visit. There were then one or two shops among the terraced houses of the side streets, and a community life arcane – though not hostile – to a couple of middle-class undergraduates. Elderly people stood at their open doors in slippers and passed the time of day, and the butcher's queue conversed in a language as mysterious to us as thieves' cant. The butcher himself for some reason was known as "Le (pronounced Lee) Capitaine".

To this abode – it wasn't really even a flat – one afternoon came Colin McLeod. My husband said, "I've invited him to tea, he always walks across to Binsey", and from then on I was privileged to be included in a friendship that lasted until Colin's untimely death in his thirties. His scholarship – he was a classicist – was universally acknowledged to be second to none, but he wore it not just lightly, he had no trace of the self-regarding or competitive air which is what many academics seemingly cannot help but breathe. And one sensed, rather than knew, that this most unassuming man was also a deeply spiritual person.

When we were trying to come to terms with our grief and shock we were by then living in Tackley; but another couple, friends of ours and his, phoned and suggested we went sliding with them, and with all our children, on Port Meadow.

It seemed an odd invitation, but it was just right. In cold winters the ice forms a layer over the flooded part of the meadow, and makes a huge, safe skating area. To be out of doors, on the move, with the children not really able to comprehend our feelings but loving the strangeness of the ice, and the freedom, and to be there where Colin had so often walked – these all helped start the long and difficult healing.

So my personal connections with Port Meadow go way back and deep, but they convince me that it acts as a rather unusual kind of *tabula rasa*, a clean slate, on which whatever you carry can be projected and forgivingly absorbed. It is less a Presence than an openness, a truly open space.

Much later, I was briefly part of a group that attempted to practise "Goethean Science". I never quite got the hang of what this was, but it involved attentive observation and no dissection, and that attracted me. We went once – the half dozen of us – on a field trip to Port Meadow, which different members of the group later told us they had experienced as "a giant Ear" and "a great Eye". I think I was trying too hard, or was rendered too sceptical by the faint air of mumbo-jumbo; but I do remember that I was awestruck and uplifted by the sight of a pair of swans in flight, by their whiteness, their great wingspan, and their whewing, powerful strokes. It's scarcely an uncommon sight, but often we are too unfocused to experience it fully, and I was grateful to the group for creating this kind of space, and, as it were, permission. There was one very unusual phenomenon though: a small chunk of rainbow upside down. To my relief, it was reported and scientifically explained in the local paper soon afterwards. I was excited to have seen it, but glad at the same time that others had seen it too, and that it hadn't been some Faustian figment of our overheated imaginations.

As I cross the bridge, on which a variegated bunch of town pigeons are sunning themselves, I glance to my left, remembering how the too-young husband and I used to rent one of the allotments – we both had rural hankerings – though I don't think we managed to produce much from it.

My legs are cold but the sun is warm on my back, as I cross the car park. A woman with an east European accent is explaining to an inquisitive boy why she is loading horse dung into the back of her car: "It's for the garden, for the vegetables!" She's pleased with her auspicious loot.

I contemplate the willow walk, along the south edge of the meadow. Two great-crested grebes are displaying their coppery spring heads, bowing in their formal way, and even uttering a hoarse croak or two. I stand gazing along the path, and a man calls over to me, wanting to help. Do I know where to go? He says the far end is very wet – he doesn't recommend it. So I set off northwards along a track that skirts the turfed outlines of a stone age site, where a woman is trying to teach her dog to fetch. He growls at the approach of two other dogs, and she reassures him repeatedly, "It's orright, it's orright, good boy…." A young woman jogs by in a bright red T-shirt. A lot of people have been drawn out by the sun, but there's room for us all, and for the dozen or more horses of different colours that inhabit here.

There seem to be molehills, and I wonder why they are so small, and soon find that they aren't molehills at all but piles of horse dung. The huge meadow is fringed with trees on all sides, and as I walk I soon come to what looks at first like a vast blue lake. This is the area that floods in winter, where we must have skated all those years ago. Today it is dotted with gulls, and at the scummy, feather-strewn edges wagtails forage up and down. A fat chestnut horse slips a little on the mud as it goes to the edge to drink. I can hear a sound – "wee-oo, wee-oo, wee-oo" – that I recognise but can't immediately place. From the east comes from time to time the sound of a train hooter, and I can see a gang of miniature orange-clad men at work on the track. Two greylags fly over with their coughing call. An off-white horse rolls on its back in a disarmingly ungainly way. It looks too old for that sort of thing: I have half a mind to join it. Now I realise what that sound is: wigeon – a great many grazing or swimming wigeon.

As usual, I badly need a pee, but Port Meadow not only has no loos till you get to Wolvercote, it has no cover at all; so I get myself through the gate into Burgess Field Nature Park, and thankfully find bushes, and no people. I have never been in here before: when I lived in Jericho it didn't exist – not as a designated Park at any rate.

The grass here is quite different, being not olive-green turf like Port Meadow, but straw-coloured and wigwammed, and full of the tall brown weeds of yesteryear. Various paths cut through it, and I choose one at random. A squirrel sits upright on a stump, nibbling something and being cute, like a kids' books illustration, and another frolics in the sunshine, leaping friskily high. There are snowdrops out, and spears of daffodils are showing, ready to burst open in a week or two.

I come to a marshy place across which two slender round trees have been laid as an improvised but not entirely practical bridge. Here and there piles of earth suggest work in progress, but happily perhaps the money that provided gates and notices and bulbs has run out, and the area can be left by and large alone. I continue to enjoy the place without other human beings, in contrast to the green pastures still visible on the far side of a hedge and ditch. There are plenty of birds though. A long-tailed tit flies across my path, which feels kind of lucky, like a black cat. It's a bird you seldom see alone, and sure enough I soon see others, and am able to watch a couple hovering and hawking for gnats – behaviour which I haven't observed in this species before. They are not especially shy birds, and I watch them at quite close quarters. There are also chaffinches, robins, blackbirds, and I hear the wheeze of a greenfinch. Through the gap I can see a few pretty teal among the wigeon on the water of the meadow. A red kite appears in the sky, turning slow, easy and powerful, bringing somehow a spice of wildness to the place, as they do to the well-manicured gardens of the Chilterns from whence they have spread out.

There is something dark on the ground ahead which I take to be a dead rook, but it turns out to be a chunk of charred wood. At a distance its flaky, sooted scales resembled feathers. Further on are the remains of a bonfire, and the odd can and bottle suggest conviviality. I can't feel too Tunbridge Wells about it: I enjoy a fire and a drink myself. I just wish they'd take the debris home. It occurs to me that most of the worst outdoor hazards for children are all brought about by humans – broken glass and rusty metal, dogshit, and barbed wire – which W.H. Hudson rightly called "man's devilish improvement on the bramble".

A new bird draws my attention. I've pretty much of an uneducated ear for music, but having slowed down in the last few years I notice more, and what once I would scarcely have registered now at least says to me,

What's this? even if I can only tell that it is something a little unfamiliar. And there it is: perched prominently on a bush and advertising itself with its spring song is a reed bunting, smart in its spring collar.

At the north end of the nature park there's one of the Blenheim Sawmill's stout, well-made gates, but alas! – the wooden walkway that should lead out from it back into the meadow is under such deep water that I wouldn't have been able to use it even if I had wellies rather than walking boots on. I lean for a while and look out at the toy village of distant Wolvercote, with a tiny bus moving through it as though at the click of a switch.

There's nothing for it but to go back to the gate I came in by, but I find a different path, so as to make a little circuit of it, and as I do I hear a high-up trilling, which I take for a lark. I gaze into the sky for some time to find that black dot that's so full of life, but only the motes on my own eyeballs, probably the penalty for unprotected log-sawing operations, and which normally I can forget all about, intrude on the spotless blue. As I move, more and more spires and steeples come into view, though in the twenty-first century their dream seems a little more disturbed.

Then I notice a meadow pipit, which will not usually perch on a bush, but apparently is – it is too early for a tree pipit. And the next thing I notice is a trilling sound – I can hear it better now – and I see the bird in its song flight, and realise that was probably what I heard before. A cloud of gnats catches the light – dashes rather than dots – and a green woodpecker flies low through the terrain and adds itself to the spring. Randy dunnocks are shivering their tails in that way they have – did you know that for all their Quakerlike plumage they are polygamous?

Back on Port Meadow once more I notice how the sun picks out the finest of gossamers netting every pile of horse dung. A few small pinkish-yellow clouds have materialised and are reflected in the blue lake. Like cygnets they are off-white, and seem to bear something of the same relation to fully-formed swan-white cumulus clouds.

I cross the first bouncy bridge and make for the seat on Fiddler's Island. Port Meadow itself has no seats at all. Some deep true instinct has prohibited picnic tables or park benches. It has to be naked so as not to be tamed. So as not to participate in our fallen condition.

My seat is standing in a good six inches of water, but is fine and dry
to park a bum on for lunch. Some alienated spirit has etched DETEST
on it. There's a lot to be angry about I agree, but today I feel more grateful
than angry, and I hope the scratchy young man will live long enough to
feel glad of a seat himself. Joggers come by, breathing easily and chatting.
They splash through without a pause, unfazed by the water: they've obviously done this before. From the other direction comes a youth in the
newest, whitest trainers ever seen outside a shop, and he can't conceal his
dismay at having to get them wet. He sits down ruefully on the far side
of the water to take them off, telling his dog Murphy how fed up he is.
A buzzard and a kestrel entertain me as I eat – that's three birds of prey
today – and I admire the squat white house opposite with its red roof and
chimney.

The weir cottage has a collection of boaty objects in the garden – poles
and pails – and on my right hand side, after I cross the second bridge, is
a row of boats moored and covered for the winter with just their dream-
bearing names showing, softer mostly than the names of racehorses, as
befits their gentler speed. Just one man is unwrapping his from its winter
shroud like an early butterfly.

I am now on the west bank of the Thames – or Isis – and at this point
in my walk I always think of the boat trip I made twenty years ago with
my daughter Phoebe and her friend Emma, three women in a boat
following Jerome K. Jerome and having the best holiday ever. If you can
find one in a second-hand shop you can read about it in *Three Women
in a Boat* – it's long out of print. You pass the path leading up to the
garden of The Perch here, such a quintessentially Oxford venue that you
almost know that you would find Morse and Lewis sitting with pint
mugs at one of their tables. (Or even, if you were really lucky, that dishy
new sergeant of Lewis's).

But I digress. Another seat here celebrates "T & B. Together 50 years."
I salute them, and pass on, but not before a kingfisher has come out of
nowhere and tingled me with its blue lightning, crossing obliquely, and
has gone. On this side of the river the grass shows the swell of ancient
ridge and furrow ploughing, and molehills are actual molehills. There are
hawthorns, and willows with watery patterns up their trunks, and descen-
dants or avatars of Hopkins' poplars. And here is something very

springlike, with long narrow bright red buds, like the penises that can suddenly and embarrassingly protrude from small dogs.

T.S. Eliot famously wrote that April was the cruellest month, but I think it is sometimes March, or just spring generally. And to me it's not cruel, which suggests agency, so much as only a little painful, because we have been gritted against the winter, and suddenly the sun is kind and we feel emotional. Because here we go again, a new leaf, a new start, and all other springs are buried in this one. And where are all those, like Colin, who aren't here to say: "Oh, look! a kingfisher."

On the far side five redshank are standing in the mud with their heads tucked in, in afternoon doze. Someone has lit a fire here too, quite a major one, more than a picnic. Perhaps they were burning cut wood as part of some riverine maintenance. The heat of the ash is still considerable and would have baked potatoes beautifully.

And here I am at Wolvercote passing the ruins of Godstow Nunnery rather quickly because the traffic noise from the main road begins to impinge on its peace, passing The Trout and still no Morse, pausing to admire the community orchard with its living treasure of old varieties of apple whose very names put heart into you – Bampton Fairing, Winter Greening, Annual Sweeting, Peggie's Pride – and past an old lady feeding the ducks.

WYCHWOOD FOREST

A general election was called today, and already in Summertown, north of Oxford, where I'm waiting for a bus, there are huge election posters, and already they have been annotated by opponents. I feel pleasantly enlivened. I had been feeling jaded about the whole business, and here, lo and behold, some fighting spirit, some political will in evidence. I have always in the past been enough of a political animal to stay up eating bacon sandwiches in the small hours and colouring in maps, but this time I felt lack-lustre. Suddenly I see now why people might want to support football teams. If you decide which lot you want to win, then the whole thing becomes more urgent and exciting. I used to have a team, but now I'm a floating voter – a disagreeable-sounding thing in itself, suggestive of corpses, or turds too light to flush away. The posters made me begin to take an interest again, to hope, to believe…

Twenty years ago I was involved in a very small way in a campaign, and that campaign had itself lasted for twenty years. Its object was to regain the right of access to the ancient forest of Wychwood. It was an unequal battle, between the wealthy landowner who could afford to fee a bigshot barrister, and walkers who had day jobs and no spare cash. But in the end the walkers won.

The term "forest" originally included many kinds of terrain, not all
with trees or even scrub. A waymarked route now explores and celebrates
the large area that was Wychwood Forest in this original sense. But the
paths we wanted back went through the woods, and the mile-and-a-half
we eventually got connected with another old route known as Patch
Riding, in the parish of Finstock. There is not much woodland walking
to be had in Oxfordshire, and none with the history and atmosphere this
track has.

I remember being nervous before my slot at the Public Enquiry, and
I remember encountering the opposition's barrister, human like me, in
the loo beforehand. She seemed to be about my own age, and although
I wasn't kitted out like a career woman I reminded myself that I had been
at Somerville and need not be intimidated. When representations were
made on behalf of the venerable Oxford Fieldpaths Society, she gave to
the word "field" a scornful emphasis, as though this could have nothing
to do with woods. What she failed, or affected to fail, to realise was the
"field" like "forest" once embraced a wider range of meaning. She wanted
too, I fancy, to imply that there was something of less consequence about
such people. At best, they were the objects of patronage, like the field
mice in *The Wind in the Willows*.

My submission stressed the importance of footpaths in our national
culture. I was appearing as an Oxfordshire walker, but also as the author
of a book called *The English Path*, and I argued that writers like
Wordsworth and painters like Constable owed a good deal to the access
that paths afforded, and that we owed a lot to such creative people. I
argued that such paths and open spaces were as necessary to the spirit as
food to the body. One of the reasons that the previous enquiry had failed
to deliver us access was that the path was no longer considered a neces-
sity – it was not used as a through route for getting from A to B but
merely for pleasure. As I tried to voice the case for a spiritual need, a
murmur of assent ran through the hall. A footpath is for the refreshment
of all of us, not just writers and artists. Nonetheless I was asked, "Would
you really walk there, to inspire your writing, if the path were opened?"
"Yes."

And over the years I have done so from time to time, and people who
live closer will have done so more often, and I am headed there today, to

one of my oases that is not only delightful and refreshing in itself, but precious for having been hard won. I like to think when I walk there of Alison Kemp and Rowland Pomfret, two doughty footpath warriors who have since died. Because of them and many others, future walkers who may not have heard their names are able to enjoy the beauty of the woods. Mollie Harris has written about Wychwood, curiously using the same epithet secret as was used by the Council for the Protection of Rural England in a pamphlet supporting the case for access. She was given special permission by Lord Rotherwick to roam there more widely, and she expresses much gratitude for the privilege, enjoins the rest of us not to trespass, but ends up by saying she hopes that someone else will write about "what is really our heritage".

The churchyard grass in Charlbury is getting its first cut, and my nostrils get a sharp hit of grass mixed with petrol, marker of the new season. Primroses are in flower all along the verges, and above the full and fast-flowing Evenlode I see the year's first swallows, although a horse is still dressed in its blanket. Shining celandines, sweet violets and vivid green dog's mercury show on the verges also, and although I'm walking along a fair-sized straight road with some fast traffic I suddenly realise I am smiling. There are white violets too, and cowslips in bud. And after half a mile there's a bench, in the middle of nowhere. I sit on it ritually for a few minutes, rather to acknowledge the thoughtfulness that put it there than out of weariness. But immediately I hear a lark which I hadn't clocked when striding along, and I watch it ascend, in short pushes as it reaches its highest point. The forest lies black across from me.

Further along the road a small stubby milestone is thickly lichened in yellow and white. It is also so weathered and eroded that all that can be made out – no numbers, no place names – is the word MILES.

The hedge here has been recently laid, with the skill that is being rediscovered and learned by a new generation hereabouts, and is even sometimes making barbed wire unnecessary, and making the countryside looked loved once more. It is just now budburst for the hawthorn leaves. Tall oaks and an ash stand in the hedge at intervals, lovely in the land-scape, needed by the birds. Another seat – this one of pretty wrought iron – and I sit once more. Behind me is tree-fringed green wold, gently undu-lating, with small settlements and fields of winter wheat. In front of me at a distance I can make out two deer grazing in a green field in front of the dark trees.

Where the road to Leafield turns off there is a hollow oak, ivy-covered, with a crow's nest in it, and a third seat. Sitting and looking back I can see that I've been coming very gently uphill, and I realise that the rise and fall of this countryside contributes greatly to its charm.

Along the smaller road I am preceded by a brimstone butterfly, threading its fluttering way through the lower branches of the flanking trees. A small deer crosses ahead of me. It pauses at the verge, not bothered by my approach, lifts its feet in a finicky fashion, flicking them, and then with a small neat bound is into the trees on the right. Among the trees there are a number of hives, some leaning and all greyish, like wooden furniture that's been out of doors a long time. I feel a touch of the sadness that arises in the presence of old, abandoned things, and then a small movement makes me look more closely. Bees! When I look through my binoculars I can see that every hive is busy. So there will be honey still for tea. I tell myself off for jumping too readily to melancholy conclusions, and walk along cheered. A three-piece suite is also in the wood, and that is quite definitely abandoned, but it has been there so long that mosses and lichens have taken hold, and are claiming it as forest furniture. You would scarcely be surprised to find Oberon and Titania sitting there, enthroned.

A wood anemone shows here and there, where some felling has opened a space. It makes me wonder if it is time to go and see if ours are out yet on Tackley Heath, and a few days later I do, and am met by a feast of delicate beauty under the misty just-leafing trees, matched perfectly with the willow warbler's fragile song. Nature's multi-media event.

Here in Wychwood is a huge lavish yellow burst of pussy willow, and there is another deer. Every so often comes a pheasant's raucous call. Traveller's joy hangs pale over the sombre trees at the miry start of the path. Finstock 2 miles, says the sign, and I enter the begrudged and canopied refuge.

It soon becomes clear from the embedded stones that the path was an old one. It is quite different from a grassy woodland "ride". A breeze gets up and sets the trees asway, so that they scrape and squeak against one another as Thomas Hardy described in *The Woodlanders*, though I don't hear it as a painful sound, as he did. The woodland floor is pale with last year's fallen leaves, through which dog's mercury has sprung up in big drifts. Bright green moss colours the still wintry trees.

A long-tailed tit gives its buzzy call, and a woodpigeon shakes its pale blue feathers and flaps clumsily away. There are other small snatches of song and calls, but the birds are difficult to see. A strange structure set back from the path, of branches fashioned like a small tent, catches my eye because of some touch of red. Looking more closely I can see that a half a dozen children's woolly toy animals have been hung up on the front of it, as though on a gamekeeper's gibbet. This is no teddy bears' picnic – they hang by the neck. Sometimes an unexpected bright colour in a wood has turned out to be the fading flowers of a memorial. Or there is an ancient thorn not far from here, at Wilcote, where small votive rags are sometimes tied accompanying half-pagan intercessions. This bit of voodoo doesn't seem quite to fit into either category.

A fallen tree with a view across to one of the forbidden green rides seems a good place for lunch, and while I eat a troupe of sun-lit pheasants entertain me in their opulent finery like strolling players. A robin whistles lonesome, and then a wren trills with its Reepicheep bravado, and the breeze is warm.

As I walk on, I am suddenly aware of someone coming up behind me. Meeting a man in a wood in broad daylight shouldn't be scary, but forest fears run deep, and there are no houses for a long way. I greet him, trying to seize the initiative.

"What are you looking for?" he asks me. "I see your notebook."

"Oh, whatever's about," I respond vaguely, trying to seem uninteresting as prey of any sort.

"I thought it might be fungi," he says with a touch of disappointment.

"I'm listening out for the birds," I give out as a partial peace offering. I loiter, and he goes on ahead, overtaking me. Soon after that I hear the chack of a great-spotted woodpecker, and then I see it, surprisingly low down on a trunk. A pussy willow is covered with several different kinds of flying insects, a horde feasting on the pollen.

The path has gentle ups and downs, and is miry in some places. In others it is dry with the old stones prominent. Sometimes it is narrow between banks, and sometimes wider and more grassy. From time to time small dark deer are visible, moving along parallel to the path and not too bothered by my presence. The breeze catches some tall pines, and makes the sound of the sea, and then in some deciduous trees produces the sound of percussion sticks, but it doesn't reach down to my skin where I walk. A movement catches my eye, and there, brownish green among brownish green twigs, to my great delight is a goldcrest. It's only the second one I've seen this year. The first was close to Jarn Mound on Boar's Hill a few weeks back. After a very hard winter one looks out anxiously for the smaller birds, and the goldcrest is the smallest. Kingfishers too suffer in the cold, and I watch out for those too. The goldcrest is not a particularly shy bird, just unobtrusive, and I am able to watch for some time as it fossicks quietly among the twigs with its tiny, buttercup blazon.

I never feel more ignorant than I do in a wood – there is so much to know. A beech carries a plate fungus so old that it has other fungi growing on it. Another has a fern growing high up in it. Everywhere there are lichens, beetles, stirrings, there is composting and bud-bursting life. As often I return to Wordsworth's gnomic pronouncements about the moral effects of nature, the supposed power of a vernal wood, and his idea that love of nature led to love of humankind. I wonder if he would feel the same if he could have seen two centuries ahead some of the things human beings have done to nature.

It's an odd claim when you think about it, but this wood is vernal alright, so I try to see if my moral compass is truer, or if I understand people any better than usual. But it's impossible to say. All I can say is that I feel better, in the sense of happier rather than more virtuous, in the way that I almost invariably do when I am out of doors amidst nature; and so any current difficulties with my fellow human beings seem eased – perhaps because they are not here, and beauty is? And then again wandering lonely is nourishing to an introvert mind, and you can face the world again in a friendlier spirit after a spell of it. But I would rather, just now, instead of introspection, stand and drink in the pearly, coral-coloured sheen of the beech buds, and marvel at how the delicate grace of the twigs contrasts with the silver-grey strength of the trunks.

The path has now itself become a wide green ride, with primroses beneath the trees at the edges, and a brimstone butterfly that flies lingeringly past just above them, as though one of them had taken wing. And all at once there is a different green under the trees, with more blue in it than the virid dog's mercury. Soon I can see – and smell – what it is: ramsons – wild garlic – big drifts of it. As I stand and take it in, it calls up strong feelings in me. One is memories of my friends Heather and Robin Tanner, both dead now, and their shared love of woodland plants, celebrated in writing, drawing and etching. Heather writes that the colour is that of young beech leaves, but to my eyes it is bluer. For some reason this plant particularly makes me remember their two strong spirits, their deep love of nature, their creativity, their hospitality.

Then another association makes itself known. My son-in-law Luke is a foreign correspondent, and just a few days ago he was writing about the garlic-pickers from a village in Chechnia called Archaty. They had permission to go into the forest to gather garlic, but the story was that they had unwittingly strayed into the middle of a counter-insurgency operation and were killed by the Russians. Two disastrous suicide bombs on the Moscow Metro were said to be in revenge for this. The contrast between the innocence and simplicity of the expedition and its bitter outcome could scarcely be more poignant: two worlds, two world-views, in collision. In England we don't usually go garlicking these days, and our wild harvestings are in general scaled down to a few stubborn refusniks of the television and supermarket culture, or gourmet enthusiasts for scarce but delectable fungi. Even blackberrying is less common. We find the berries inexplicably wizened and inedible, we are worried about toxic sprays, or we simply can't be bothered. Those young Chechen garlic pickers speak to our rural past. I stood for a while by the patch of ramsons thinking of them. I would have liked to pray. I'm not sure this was the kind of impulse Wordsworth had in mind, but I went on my way sobered, grateful for life in the midst of so much beauty – and for a flawed but still a relatively flourishing democracy.

At the place where you can press your face against the wire and look back along a wide stream's meanders there is a buzzard circling low, and from inside the forbidden wood a jay's harsh call sounds. The route that is opened once a year on Palm Sunday, so that we can fill our bottles with "licky water" (water flavoured with liquorice) at the spring, allows us to walk beside the stream, and the excitement is always to try to see and hear the mating toads. The fence is too much for an oldie like me, but if I did come over all Robin Hood and decide to go in there, I would probably, if caught, get told off, but not shot. "Please trespass," wrote the poet Edward Thomas, who was killed fighting for England, at the very end of the war to end all wars. I wish I had the courage to more often.

The colours are subdued, as they usually are in England, so that the blue of distant woodsmoke and a speckling of bright orange fungus on a branch contrast agreeably, and seem dramatic. A pair of marsh tits are chasing each other in a very springlike fashion among early, just-opened hazel leaves as the path emerges into an open field. And there's a dark butterfly – possibly a peacock. Yes, it settles and I can see the circles on its wings.

And here is that man, coming back again. I am pleased because I have decided he was harmless, and have wished to atone for my caution.

"Are you interested in fungi?" I ask him, and he replies that he has a book back at home, but finds it hard to identify things. We agree that specimens which must surely seem obvious when we look them up back at the ranch never are, and we both confess our timidity about ever picking any to eat. He asks what birds I've seen, and I tell him how pleased I was to see the goldcrest.

"Do you know a goldcrest?" He says he does, but looks a tad unimpressed, as though he is humouring me. Perhaps he thinks I mean a goldfinch, and has a garden full of them, as I have. But as we go our separate ways I feel a little better, having, I hope mutually, a little amended our view of human nature.

My walk ends with a strawberry ice cream from the Finstock village shop, eaten on a bench in the sun as I wait for the bus.

TACKLEY HEATH

The cuckoo greets me as I step inside the Heath, and thrills me, as always. A furtive bird with a disreputable lifestyle, why does it announce its presence so unmistakably, and why do we humans feel so gladdened by its annual return?

Welcome as are all the signs of spring in our deepest psyche, continually wanting renewal and rebirth, there is something physical in its appeal also. A cool, edgy bell that carries a long way, there is nothing at all like it, and everyone knows it. It has more or less lost its old association with the shame and pain of cuckoldry, but still it is a maverick voice, a loner's, overriding other voices, other lives. Perhaps it is the sound of primal selfishness, of the unsocialised free spirit that all of us would-be-goods need to reconnect with from time to time – a note that in a bird we are allowed not to disapprove of. And now that the cuckoo seems to be less common, for reasons that we don't understand although they are likely to be our doing, we value it even more, and hear it with relief: the world is not yet totally out of kilter. My friend Judy phones me excitedly towards the end of May to say that she has finally heard one, at 6.20 a.m., in her garden. She is a pianist, and she tells me she is sure that the interval is a minor third, and not, as the old German composers often made it in their children's music primers, a major.

I have stood on Tackley Heath at dusk with the moon rising, a huge old apple tree in blossom glowing palely and shedding its innocent, nostalgic scent and a cuckoo calling, and I have felt like a trespasser in an alien world, it was so weirdly beautiful. I have also stood on the Heath soon after dawn with the composer Robert Sherlaw Johnson, the late husband of my friend Rachael who has illustrated this book, for him to teach me the songs of the different warblers. Like Messiaen, whose work he admired, Robert sometimes incorporated birdsong into his music. I have an indifferent ear, and still struggle with the songs, but it was instructive to stand there with someone so unworldly. He had a bird book tucked under his arm, and several times, as he became rapt, it slipped and fell to the ground, and he (paying scant attention to practicalities especially during the music of a dawn chorus) would retrieve it and hold it in just the same way, and in just the same way it would fall once more.

It's many years since I visited the heath with Robert, and since then I have improved my knowledge a little – a very little, and slowly. I can hear a thrush, which is cheering. They too are fewer in number than they were. There are also chaffinches, robins, a blackbird, and a chiffchaff. Somewhere in the hedge is a scratchy whitethroat. As I penetrate further in there are other chiffchaffs, a blackcap or two, great and blue tits. It is mid-morning, but there is still a soft, rich tapestry of song.

Tackley Heath is not a heather-and-gorse heath, but an area of bracken which can be wandered through on a number of fairly random and shifting paths, that come and go with the seasons and people's habits. At quiet times you can glimpse a deer stock-still at a distance among the trees. At most times of year you find a wigwam or two – or the lacy brown remains of them – made by children. They are a reassuring sight in these cautious indoor times. (I am as guilty as any, feeling more relaxed when my grandchildren are reading or at the computer than when they are, for example, at the high top of our unpollarded garden willow. Once recently I heard the heart-stopping cry of "Gran, I'm stuck!" and luckily found my younger, feistier neighbour Jane at home, and kindly willing to climb up and assist in the descent…).

Some of the Heath is open and some covered with trees – the majority oaks being of all shapes and sizes – and bushes. You can enter it from a minor road by one of three or four gaps in the hedge, from whence soft narrow trails lead off into the mystery, and it's easy to lose your bearings; or you can enter at the southern corner by way of a fieldpath. This is my favourite way in. A stout oak stands there, older than most of the others, and the path leads in past a drift of yellow archangels, a wood violet or two, and an old, abandoned galvanised pail.

In April the Heath is ethereally beautiful, with the budburst of some early green leaves and the delicate pale wood anemones in profusion, and a few plants of the even purer and more vernal wood sorrel with its bright green trefoils; but it is most glorious and most loved in May when some of the sky seems to have fallen and the bluebells are out. They stretch away in all directions, darker and more mysterious in the shade under the trees (which appear to be standing in water), cheerful and prodigal on the open heath. No way is this blue the colour of low spirits. And as though the sight alone was not enough to seduce you away from worldly preoc-cupations, the soft, uncloying scent stays active one's nostrils, unlike some fragrances that anaesthetise your sense so that you soon cease to be aware of them.

The hawthorn blossom is just beginning to open but does not yet dominate, either in scent or sight. Instead the dainty, starry stitchwort gives a visual counterpoint to the blue. Last year's dead bracken is a soft light brown, and this year's is beginning to be green, its crooks well up, but still with curled and rusty tips. Later in the year it becomes tall, coarse and pretty well impenetrable, and the bluebells then nowhere to be seen. But now the paths are perfect, dry and springy from year upon year of dried bracken and leaf-mould, and from an otherwise rather disastrous lack of spring rain.

I sit for a while on a piece of cut oak trunk at the base of a fellow that has survived. Some of the oaks are stag-horned, some have at some time been coppiced, and some are perfect domes of yellow-green. Simon Schama spoke on Radio Four recently warning of something that threat-ened to wipe out the oak as effectively as the bark beetle did the elm. He urged whichever party won the election to pour money into research to prevent this from happening, implying I think that apart from anything else the symbolism of an oakless England would be devastating. A natu-ralist friend said that he was talking through his hat. I hope so. Because, forget the symbolism, it would mean the beauty not only of this small heath but that of much of rural England would be devastated. In a heart-felt passage, the great nature writer Richard Jefferies wrote that he wanted to bring factory workers to sit under an oak. He felt it would restore their souls. I would like to bring financiers and cabinet ministers too.

Though it is not an unalloyed idyll, sitting here. I anxiously unscrew my new insect repellent, trying to work out how to apply it without getting it on any of the parts it must not be applied to, such as my eyes. It's the season of the dreaded Blandford fly, and in past years I've had prolonged problems both with those bites and ant bites. The Blandford season is only a few weeks long, but they are weeks which I can't possibly spend indoors. A few yards away a small birch is wound about with honeysuckle like ribbons round a Maypole and a-dance with a host of winged insects. Some look like mayflies, with their long tail filaments and bouncing movement spending their single day, but there are several different kinds of flying creature, some smaller, some larger, some peaceful, some frenetic. Probably not all are interested in my blood, but I don't care to test it. And just then begins another kind of hum – the sound of a power saw.

It seems to come from the clearing, a place where there is rough circle of trees, without undergrowth, where village barbecues are held to mark the beginning of spring, with breakfast sausages cooked alfresco. By the time I get there a good-sized oak has been cut down and cut up into effi-cient pieces, and is being taken away in barrow loads. I sit on a fallen tree and watch for a bit.

"Was there something wrong with the tree?" I ask finally. (You don't unnecessarily antagonise a guy with a chainsaw.)

"Dead," he answers laconically.

I refrain from saying, "Well, it is now," though the sliced-through bole looks as sound as a bell, and shows no signs of rot. One or two of the branches may have been dead, but oaks can last long after they have been partially hollowed out.

The fact is, though, the man is within his rights, provided he lives in the parish, because Tackley Heath is what is known as a fuel allotment, which means that parishioners are allowed to cut whatever they like. At one time this was mainly bracken – or furze as it was called – and any trees that sprang up would not attain any great size. With increasing prosperity and the decrease in the number of open fires, the trees grew larger. Now we are set to become poor again, and wood-burning stoves are in fashion, and there are others like me who scavenge fallen branches and trees, mainly any dead elms that are still around. But the wood-burners don't do well with unseasoned timber, and I can't help hoping his chimney will tar up on him.

In the fork of another of the oaks is a bunch of fresh flowers, and a small brass plate that records another untimely death, of a young woman much loved in the village. "I'm a fiery fairy full of life" it reads, touchingly and memorably.

Elsewhere on the Heath I meet a second guy with a Ray Mears complex. He looks less convincing than the tree-feller. He has a rather new-looking leather holster affair with a couple of knives stuck in it, over a very neat shirt and trousers. He looks like a recently-retired desk-worker. He greets me and then goes somewhat self-consciously or circumspectly by, staring about him. I'm curious. What can he be hoping to harvest? Truffles? Later I come on him again and catch him in the act – stuffing nettles into a plastic sack.

"For the compost," he offers, though I didn't ask.

"Good for you," I say, and can hardly forbear laughing. He must have such a tidy suburban garden to have no home-grown nettles. He can come and get mine any time. But I suspect it is more about a fantasy of hunting and gathering.

Wandering on I can glimpse through the trees Old Man Leys farm and its pastures, with three chestnut horses and the sheep with this year's lambs. One of the sheep has found her way through the thorn hedge into the Heath with her two lambs trotting behind. She looks suitably dishevelled, and her lambs pull anxiously on her udders each time she stops to browse.

I am watching long-tailed tits through my binoculars when I am startled by a young woman with a dog who comes up behind me. She apologises for making me jump, and asks if I have seen the cuckoo.

"We almost did," she says. "We came quite close."

And it comes back to me that I once was obsessed with that same quest, following the sound and hoping to see the bird. In my experience the bird is hard to see if you pursue it, but it will sometimes appear when you are not expecting it, when your concentration is relaxed – rather like a name you've given up trying to recall, or the answer to a crossword clue. And it happens today – as I am sitting and watching small greyish aphids crawl on sticky sycamore leaves, and marvelling, with a dash of disgust, at the strangeness and diversity of life – the sly, lanky thing goes silently across the space between the trees. There's something just a touch reptilian about a cuckoo, to my eyes, recalling genetic origins in prehistory. And the bracken too is snaky, its heads bent over like cobras, and there are even some viperish, dark markings on the stems.

Here and there a butterfly goes ahead of me. I recognise the easy ones: pretty orange-tips, and dark opulent peacocks. There are bees too, both bumbles and smaller, tawny-arsed ones. A pheasant takes off in a flurry. Unseen cobwebs tickle my face. I've seen a kestrel hovering, and a buzzard or two at a height, but here suddenly is a different raptor circling in the blue space between the trees, its forked tail showing it to be a red kite. This bird is new to the parish. It settles on one of the tall oaks across the muddy ditch that marks the boundary between the Heath and a private wood, and I'm able to study its small fierce face and hooked beak. Then a second bird circles also, and settles not far off, and for the next half hour I watch as they both fly, but not far, and not high, showing their fox-coloured feathers, and settle again. I wonder if they are a pair, and if they are nesting, or considering it. I'm told later the farmer is aware of them, and worried about his lambs. As I understand it he need not be, though they may be interested in a dropped afterbirth.

A great spotted woodpecker is banging away at an already much-pecked pine tree at the wood's edge; and here's a treat – a treecreeper, a bird I can never be sure I will see but that I am granted from time to time, like an unexpected quiet blessing. Their colouration is not unlike certain waders, subtle and intricate brown striations on the back, and silky pale underneath, like the cap of a field mushroom.

My third scavenger is an elderly lady. Definitely a lady, not a woman. What she is wearing would do equally well for the Bridge Club. But she is sitting in the low fork of a tree, and in her hand is a small camera. She wants to make off with the bluebells, to take the spring captive, just like I do.

"Aren't we lucky?" we ask each other.

Lucky, yes, and because human sinful, as all we steppers into Eden.

HOOKY CUTTING

As the bus takes me through the ironstone villages – all with the same foxy stone but each with its own character – I have a vision of life lived in a steady, time-honoured way in villages all over England. It's an illusion of course: few people work on the land any more, or in the villages where they live. The year before last I worked on the organic farm in North Aston and it was one of the toughest and most rewarding jobs I ever did. At the end of each day I would be sweaty and soiled and soaked or sunburned, every muscle painful, and have a broad beam of satisfaction on my face. I wish I could take the sad young people with their dogs and begging bowls from the doorways of Oxford and show them what the good life can be like. But I realise that in some mysterious way my pleasure is an outcome of my privilege. Though I didn't have that much choice of work: I was turned down (thank goodness!) by both Marks and Spencer and Sainsbury's. I failed to get a simple simple sum right at the interview, plus I suspect my hair and nails were not ladylike.

Never idyllic, and in many ways altered for the better, rural life is still a-changing. But we English do continue to love our gardens, and in the country we are still very aware of the signs of the changing seasons. I know from my own village a little of what the picture postcard doesn't show. I can remember walking through Tackley early one morning and thinking of the various sadnesses I knew lurked under the quiet slate roofs and behind the hollyhocked stone walls.

But those of us who choose country life cannot but be aware of the relief when we step off the bus into the sounds of pigeons cooing and blackbirds playing their rustic pipes, and the scents from gardens of lilac or roses, and even in summer, the few degrees cooler than Oxford or Banbury, where the heat beats up from the pavement and stews between bodies and buildings.

Today, towards midsummer, the countryside is very soft-looking and green, after rain the day before. The sun is beginning to burn through a light grey cloud cover. The chestnut candles have gone over, and cow parsley has spread its dainty yet robust lace along every verge, and the occasional unsprayed field is full of buttercups, lifting the heart. It is a huge treat to sit here looking out at the rural scene, carried for free with my bus pass – a huge yet simple pleasure. My spirit begins to open out, to relax a grim control. I relish my smallness in the scheme of things. My worries seem to abate and shrink to a manage-able size. The bus fills up as we go along. Hardly anyone gets off: we are all going to Banbury.

Once there I dip briefly into the urban world while waiting for the bus to Hook Norton. I notice particularly a young black guy on his own in charge of a pushchair. He walks with great bouncy swaggering strides even though – or perhaps because – he is a dad. The bus station pigeons too seem to swagger a little, and who can blame them when the sea-green iridescence on their necks is such that you would consider it vulgar even in a kids' tube of Christmas glitter.

The next bus takes me out into red earth and less familiar territory. It goes by way of Bloxham and Milcombe. I have never heard of Milcombe. A county is vast: there is so much to explore. And every village in it has footpaths and hidden twittens, greens, churches, chapels, pubs, streams, revelations, riches. Hook Norton when we get there is struggling with delivery lorries and the bus is the last straw. For a moment it seems a busy place, but within a few minutes, as I get my bearings, it all resolves itself. Village streets weren't made for these huge vehicles.

I'm headed for the BBOWT nature reserve in an old railway cutting. It's great to have a nature reserve, but I can't help thinking that whatever was in those lorries would be better on a goods train, something that might have been more possible without all the line closures… I set out as the book instructs me on the minor road to Swerford – and everyone I pass greets me. It's so striking that I think for a moment or two that I must be the double of someone who lives there. But no, it's the Hook Norton way, the good opposite of a vicious circle: I begin to expect to be greeted pleasantly, and so my own face opens out and looks more friendly, making such greetings more likely…

There's an attractive, lichened old seat on the outskirts of the village, slightly longer than usual, wooden, but with curled wrought iron bands. It is showing its age just a little, and I sit on it carefully, with respect. Some villages would have junked it already, and put a hard modern one with no soul in its place.

Having taken a few minutes to enjoy the view across a dip to tree-edged pastures, and to pick out, as well as the benign summery ring-doves, the sounds of blackbird, chiffchaff, song-thrush, and wren, I carry on up the road. It's turning into a hot day, and by the time I think I must have gone too far, I am beginning to sweat. I slow right down. Impatience to arrive, I know from experience, is almost always counter-productive. I retrace my steps. Back at the seat again I cast about until I see some people. There may have been plenty of people about before, but it's a rule that they will all have vanished when you need to ask the way, or where the bus stops, or whatever. Finally I spot some in their garden, and I approach the natives confidently, certain that Hook Norton looks kindly on the stranger. And as I guessed they do know the way. One of the women gives me detailed directions, involving, at one point "the holey road". "I mean," she glosses smilingly, "the road with potholes in!" It was as though she appreciated that a walker's road, with a latent sense of pilgrimage, can also, at the same time, be holy. I thank her and press on, and remember at least the first few turns. I pass a small, intensely turquoise eggshell on the ground, and every now and then in the hedge an intensely pink campion. And here is a cool-looking Green-veined white, like a butterfly halfway to becoming a plant.

Wandering on I come to the conclusion that I have once again over-shot. I can see the old stone stanchions of the railway among the trees, and this track is leading me away from them. Turning back I ask again, and although I still fail to spot the notice that was mentioned I finally plunge off along a narrow and rather dank path under the trees, and soon start to see the abundant hart's tongue ferns that are one of the reserve's specialities. According to *Flora Britannica* railways often provide these with a suitably damp and shady habitat.

The reserve is in two parts, but we are energetically warned that they don't connect, that the tunnel is privately owned and unsafe. This half is wooded, and the other half is grassier and more open, with a variety of wild flowers and birds. There are a few flowers here, of the sort that will grow in deep shade, and there is one in particular that I have only just learned to identify: herb bennet. For years it has been established in my garden close to the drain from the kitchen sink, which occasionally over-flows. I liked its foliage and habit, though I had no idea what it was, and (never needing much excuse not to weed) I let it stay. The flowers are pretty, with their interspersed sepals, but insignificant, and the five small glossy yellow petals drop quickly. I had always been meaning to look it up, and always forgetting. Finally I had, and found to my great delight that its name is a corruption of *benedicta*, so that it means the blessed plant. Further, its roots, which I was told smell of cloves, were thought to have the power of protecting a house against the devil. I suppose since I don't believe in God any more I don't believe in the devil either. But I'm as superstitious as ever, and still mutter an embarrassed (if anyone else is around) greeting to a single magpie, which is said to avert the bad luck of it, and am pleased if a black cat crosses my path. More seriously, I liked the idea that this plant I had ignorantly spared year after year had an agreeable, potent-sounding folklore belonging to it, and that our house was under its protection. I dug out one small piece of it, so that I could sniff the root, and it did smell of cloves, but softly and warmly, like a clove pink.

Maybe it was the herb bennet that got me out in one piece. Because almost at once I hear a sound ahead of me that I can't place. It's a kind of tapping, or rapping, but isn't quite right for a woodpecker. Soon I begin to be able to see movements in the foliage, close to one of the great grey stanchions, so I stop to look through the binoculars. It begins to seem like something quite large, but deer are not so noisy or unwary. All at once I realise there's another human being in there, half-hidden, performing some kind of energetic movements. I'm not sure what he's doing, or if it is a he, but I become aware that I'm looking at whoever it is through binoculars and that it's inappropriate to spy thus on one's own species. (I have sometimes even felt this about the others.) "Oh!" I exclaim, half-involuntarily, loud enough to be heard, and then I beat it. I don't say sorry because I may not have been seen and I don't want to be, and with my heart hitting my gullet I crack along the suddenly distinctly Gothic path, hoping it will take me somewhere out of here, somewhere where, as George Eliot had a rustic put it in *Adam Bede* "there's finger-poasses, an' folks to ax the way on."

I emerge onto the same minor road I originally took. If I had persevered a very short way further I would have come to the BBOWT notice I'm now standing by, and entered from the other end. The Trust's notices are always low-key, set back a little from the road, and often overhung with leaves. I don't know if this is policy, so that the casual visitor isn't encouraged, but it certainly heightens the sense of achievement and so probably the appreciation you feel when you do find the place.

I decide that whatever activity was occupying that still unseen person I am not really that excited by ferns. I do not care for dark woods and lumpish grey pillars. I would rather find the other, the flowery, half. So I copy the map on the interpretation board very carefully into my notebook, and commence road walking once again with a sense of liberation. Usually I prefer a path, but for once I feel quite warmly towards the tarmac that, though there is scarcely any traffic, definitely goes somewhere, and I enjoy the quiet ring of my boots, and the tall hedges full of birds.

Soon I pass a notice on a farm gate. The good news is it says Tunnelside Farm, which suggests I'm going the right way. The bad news: "Dangerous Guard Dogs". I never quite believe people even when they gratuitously explain that their dogs are harmless: "methinks the lady doth protest too much...". But these dogs are actually billed as dangerous. Not that I can see dogs of any sort. However, being as you will by now have realised of an anxious disposition, and not at all resembling those desperado, stop-at-nothing naturalists I imagine the notice is aimed at – the picturesque but rusting bits of farm machinery don't look worth a lot so it can't be that – I proceed by the long way round. A blackcap in good voice from an elder tree cheers me on my way, and I can hear a drumming woodpecker, a creaky yellowhammer's song and the soft ripple of a willow warbler. Black bryony has wound itself round a gate and is sending out its shining, snaky heads in search of something else to embrace. There is plenty to look at without trespassing into dangerous dog-infested tunnels.

A signpost says that Great Rollright is only two-and-a-half miles away. The oddly uncountable old stones with their legends and wide views will have to wait for another day. I feel wistful for a moment, tempted to expand my range, until I remember how I am scratching the surface only, drinking a few drops from a deep well, and how there is more, much more, than a person can truly take in, in one lifetime. Look deep enough, and that is true of any village, any meadow even.

As I get closer to the entrance a family are coming away. The adults greet me in a foreign accent, and the kids do not greet me at all, but look a little sulky, as young teens usually feel honour-bound to do, even if the expedition has been fun. I decide they are Dutch. The Dutch are ahead of us in doing worthy nature things with their kids.

When I reach the cutting there is no-one else there, and I meet no-one during my entire visit. The actual line of the track is grassy, but ahead looks overgrown in places, so I decide the narrow paths people have made on either side along the top of the bank will be a better bet. The midday heat is getting more intense, trapped in a narrow channel sheltered from any breeze. I pluck a big butterbur leaf to be an insect-whisk. A may-tree has oddly various flowers, some pinkish and some white – for all the world like a white garment dyed patchily by a rogue sock in the washing-machine. Almost at once I see two or three of the promised blue butterflies, and the prettiness and abundance of the flowers make my heart almost painfully glad. There are vetches, plantains with flowery skirts, and ox-eye daisies. There are many that I can't immediately identify, but as I get older I am becoming more reconciled to the fact that I may never get round to it, and that seeing them is enough. The pleasure of identification is still considerable though, and I don't share John Fowles's view that naming is a kind of trapping. To me rather it seems like an honouring, a taking the trouble to get to know. But today simple delight, even ignorant delight, is coming into its own.

And then there is nostalgia – the flowers take me back to other summers in places half-forgotten, with people who are no longer around, of careless youth among the flowers of the Cherwell meadows, that won't come again. I have to get a handle on this emotion and not let it dampen the present. I put it to myself that other summers have brought me to the appreciation I have of this one.

The sight of the tender coral-pink of sainfoin – holy-hay – warms my thoughts. Looking is almost like eating. And speaking of food, everywhere are the fresh yellow, crimson-tipped blossoms of eggs-and-bacon. This place is not as I had expected. It is more overgrown, less visited, wilder. There are no seats, and I need to find somewhere to sit and eat my actual lunch. Added to this, the little trail I am on has all-but petered out, and I am pushing through brambles and treading down nettles on the edge of a drop that seems almost (to my temperament) vertiginous. Ahead I can see the overgrown grille behind which is the forbidden tunnel. On the other bank is a fairly open place where it might be possible to sit. But first I have to get down onto the track and up again. Big sharp railway stones are loosely piled with no view to my putting my weight on them safely, and they are half-smothered in vegetation. If I break an ankle here it might be a long time until someone else turned up. Slipping and swearing and sweating I manage it, and up the other side. I choose a thistle-free patch, avoid what might be a grassed-over anthill, and spread out *Where to Go for Wildlife* to sit on as a rudimentary defence against crawly things. My arm turns out to be bleeding freely from a scratch I didn't realise I had, and I hastily spit and dab at it, before it invites insect attention. Then I fall on my sandwich feeling I've earned it. My drink is tap water with a sprig of garden mint in it – transformative.

As I eat, the small birds get used to my presence and go about among the branches of the trees at the top of the cutting, but tantalisingly fast, as small birds do among summer leaves, so that it's hard to identify them. Finally I get my binoculars on one that's in the shade on a bare length of oak branch, and to my delight when the colour shows clear it is a bullfinch, and it starts to feed a young one perched nearby. I catch sight suddenly of the host of gnats that are in urgent motion just above my hat, but they don't seem to be biting, and I try to stay cool – sweat is always a draw – and forget they are there. A treecreeper flies in and onto a birch, its belly very like the silvery bark.

When I come to leave, a few yards further on I see with a slight shock that flies are gathered round what I at first take for a fox's tail. It is tawny brown with a black tip. Looking closer I see there are bloody bones, and the brown thing is not a tail but the lower part of a deer's leg, the black tip being the hoof.

On the way back I keep to the same bank, picking a leaf or two of wild marjoram as I go, to rub between my fingers and sniff. Finally I move down into the central track where I would probably have fared better from the start. At this point it is filled with a mass of blue speedwell. And here's one of those red and green moths – is it a cinnabar or a six-spot burnet? A better naturalist told me how to distinguish them, but of course I have forgotten. I enjoy it anyway.

Back out on the wide-verged narrow roads I plod gently back towards Hooky. A skylark is singing. The first hedge-roses are just beginning to come out. I pull one down towards me and inhale its innocent scent. I can see the orange-tawny church tower set in its flock of roofs below me. As I come into the village swifts are criss-crossing the blue sky, and a white chicken wanders across in front of me.

"Hello, there!" says a robust-looking old man in a hat, as he unloads something from a van. "Gorgeous day!"

The church is cool. A young woman quietly sweeping smiles at me as I unlace my boots and pad in, but doesn't speak or approach me in case I want to pray. I try to make out a fragment of old wall-painting. It shows curves and tufts – fish? seaweed? grass? Something from nature definitely. At one time religion was all bound up with it – leaves in the stone carvings, blessing the crops, ineluctably pagan branches at all the festivals.

I wander along the street until I come to The Pear Tree. There's plenty of time before my bus. Sitting in the garden out back with a glass of Hook Norton ale I feel I am in the right place at the right time, and completely present. Gorgeous day.